CHINESE
Takeaway
COOKBOOK

STARTERS & SOUPS

CHICKEN & DUCK

SEAFOOD

BEEF & PORK

VEGETARIAN

26.

RICE & NOODLES

58.

91.

BUNS & SWEET THINGS

135.

INTRODUCTION

'Man who stands on hill with mouth open will wait a long time for roast duck to drop in.'

Chinese food has long been a favourite weekend treat, with entire families ritualistically ordering their favourite dishes from their local Chinese every Friday night. It could quite easily be the 11th commandment: 'Thou shalt have Chinese every Friday'!

This cookbook isn't my interpretation of what I think Chinese food should taste like – this book is the holy grail of Chinese takeaway (and restaurant) trade-secret recipes. Everyone has a favourite dish and this book will help you to re-create those dishes step-by-step with ease and simplicity.

I literally grew up in the kitchens of Chinese restaurants. Unlike other children on my estate, my playground was the kitchen store room and, when it was closed, under the tables in my dad's Cantonese restaurant. I'm sure if you cut me in half it would say '10 minutes' through the middle (in a broad Chinese accent), which is pretty much what we told every customer who asked how long their order would take to arrive.

Most classic Chinese recipes cook in minutes, therefore there is some preparation to be done before we get our kwok (I mean wok!) on. Careful chopping is a must as you need to ensure that all meat and vegetables are cut uniformly, so everything can cook evenly. Seasoning and sauces also need to be pre-measured because as soon as you fire up that wok, it's all hands on deck and go, go, go! Well, for

5 minutes at least. Then it's back to the calm and you can savour the smells of the aromatics as they fill your kitchen before you sit down to eat.

Grandad, like many Chinese back in the 1950s, opted to migrate to the UK, a journey that took a month by boat, and on arrival he headed to the Midlands where he settled in Leicester. In 1962 Grandad opened Leicester's first Chinese restaurant (a chop suey house). Chinese ingredients were very hard to come by, so the menu mainly consisted of British dishes like steak and roast chicken with a few beansprouts or chop suey vegetables thrown in. The restaurant was very popular and was even visited by the Beatles when they played in Leicester in 1964.

Dad managed the restaurant for the family until 1978 when he opened his own restaurant, The Bamboo House, Leicester's very first Cantonese Restaurant. He sourced two amazing chefs from London and the business took off with a BOOM!

As you can imagine, it was hard work and took up most of my parents' time, so in 1983 they bought a restaurant on Fosse Road North in Leicester, which he named The Panda, with living accommodation above; this allowed them to spend more time with us, 'The Wan Children'. Little did I know at the time, but this would be the start of my career as a chef. Every weekend and sometimes midweek I would be in the kitchen helping, washing up, peeling prawns or chopping vegetables. It was our way of life and fuelled my obsession with food.

Dad liked that the restaurant was family-run and would often parade us around in front of the diners. There were even times when we sang carols at the tables to regular customers (much to my horror now). At 16, I left school and assumed my role as a full-time chef at The Panda. My days were spent preparing ingredients for the night ahead and in the evenings I created amazing Cantonese and Szechuan dishes. Business was booming; we even made it into **The Good Food Guide**, where we stayed for several years.

Over the years I've run a full-time Kung Fu school, presented a huge martial arts and fitness show, opened a truckers' cafe, a Taiwanese bubble tea store and a Hong Kong street food bar, yet, despite my many varied business activities over the years, cooking has always remained at the heart of my DNA. It's as natural as breathing and I cannot remember a time when I couldn't cook. I feel so lucky to have been able to share my knowledge in a myriad of magazines and newspapers, on the radio, at live events and even on TV, and now via the pages of this book – the ultimate guide to re-creating your favourite Chinese takeaway and Cantonese restaurant dishes at home!

Chinese cooking is frantic and it can feel like a workout as everything happens all at the same time, but with a little bit of TLC and forward planning you'll be tossing your wok like a pro and creating amazing dishes. In the time it takes to dial the number and order your favourite Chinese meal, you could be sitting at the table delving into rich aromatic soups, munching on crispy fried delights and shovelling down the tastiest chow mein dish you've ever eaten, all cooked by your own fair hands.

Now less of the chit-chat; get your (K)wok on and enjoy!

Kwoklyn x
www.kwoklynwan.com

CHINESE FOOD ETIQUETTE & CUSTOMS

'The kitchen is the heart of the home.'

Chinese people have many customs and traditions, such as 'you must always respect your elders' and 'the littlest of actions have huge significant meanings'. Over the years I have not always got these right and have been told off by my grandma and dad on many occasions. Even now, Dad will correct me on the smallest of things, so much so that it's now just expected and often laughed about.

- After pouring tea, it is essential never to point the spout of the teapot at others because this gesture has the same meaning as using the finger to point, which in Chinese culture is considered rude. Therefore, the spout must be directed to where no one is sitting, usually outward from the table.

- It is customary to serve fish at Chinese New Year as it symbolises 'surplus and prosperity'. This dish is normally served with a pair of serving chopsticks.

- When presented with a bowl of rice, receive it with both hands as it marks a sign of respect. Receiving with only one hand signals laziness or disrespect.

- Chinese meals are usually served on a Lazy Susan to make family-style eating all the easier. When a dish is served, the most senior person gets first dibs and then it's rotated around the table. It is polite only to take a small portion to make sure everyone gets some.

- Under no circumstances should chopsticks be placed upright in your bowl. This symbolises death.

- Be prepared for your Chinese host to place food in your bowl, usually without even asking. The host will often put chicken legs or other choice parts of the meal in the guest's bowl. Though Westerners may see this as interfering with one's independence and personal space, it is a sign of hospitality in China.

- The guest is always seated at the 'head' of the table, customarily furthest from the door, with any fish, chicken or duck heads pointing their way.

- Chinese attach particular meanings to certain foods based on shapes, colours and legends. Superstition and tradition dictate that certain foods must be eaten for certain festivals and events to invoke a blessing. For example, ingot-shaped dumplings mean wealth at New Year and round mooncakes represent family reunion in mid-autumn.

- The invention of chopsticks reflects the wisdom of ancient Chinese people. A pair of chopsticks, although they look simple, can nip, pick, rip and stir food. Nowadays, chopsticks are considered to be lucky gifts for marriage and other important ceremonies.

CANTONESE CUISINE

Cantonese cuisine originates from the Guangdong Province of China. From this major trading area, the cuisine rapidly spread throughout China and into Hong Kong, to America in the 1850s as Chinese immigrants flocked to build the Transcontinental Railroad, then into England and Europe in the 1950s and '60s with the mass migration of Chinese immigrants, especially those from rural villages who came to the West for a better way of life. Chinese food, especially Cantonese food, has become a favourite ethnic cuisine. Not just tasty, this style of cooking is far healthier than other popular delivery foods, with many stir-fries containing fewer calories and lots more vegetables.

The Holy Trinity of aromatics features heavily in Cantonese cooking – garlic, ginger and spring onion – and whether used alone or combined, they allow the chef to produce tasty yet delicate flavours.

An authentic Cantonese chef's goal is to preserve the food's original flavour. Unlike other Chinese styles of cooking, such as Szechuan where the cook buries the food in a lot of spices, a Cantonese chef aims to draw out or highlight the original flavour of the vegetable, meat or fruit.

The Chinese believe that food, besides being an absolute necessity for existence, is one of the few pleasures that span the entirety of our lives. For this reason, the joy of eating is given huge importance. Chinese people pay great attention to the colour, smell, taste, texture and shape of their food; the taste is regarded as the soul of Chinese food. There are five main flavours, which can be categorised as salty, spicy, sour, sweet and bitter, and recently umami has been added to this list. Mastering how to combine the flavours harmoniously improves taste.

Top tip! If you want just a hint of their aroma, cut the aromatics into larger pieces and add them at the beginning of cooking, whether stir-frying, steaming or poaching. The large pieces will gently flavour the dish and can then be easily picked out while eating. For a bolder flavour, finely chop or grate the aromatics: their greater distribution during the cooking process will allow more of their flavour to enter the dish, adding intensity.

SZECHUAN CUISINE

Szechuan cuisine originates from southwestern China's Sichuan province, a region famous for bold flavours, especially its generous use of garlic and spices. Renowned ingredients used are dried chillies and Szechuan peppercorns which produce a distinct spicy and mouth-numbing taste sensation. Due to the very wet climate, Szechuan cuisine specialises in preserving techniques such as drying, salting and pickling.

CHINESE COOKING TECHNIQUES

'Cooking is LOVE made visible.'

Stir-frying

A Chinese cooking technique where ingredients are fried in a small amount of oil in a very hot wok. Originating in China it rapidly spread throughout Asia along the trading routes across the old Silk Road. The benefits of stir-frying include the use of very little oil, which makes the food low in fat and calories, and the high heat cooks the food quickly, retaining its nutrients.

It is important to prepare all recipe ingredients in advance – once cooking starts there will be no time for chopping. Ensure all your ingredients are chopped evenly, allowing everything to be cooked at the same time. Once the food is in the wok, you need to flip it regularly to avoid burning and sticking to the bottom of the wok. Use a ladle, wooden spoon or spatula to scoop the food efficiently.

Serve the food immediately after cooking or the ingredients will lose their natural texture and flavour.

Steaming

A traditional Chinese cooking technique that uses very little to no oil, wonderful for preparing healthy dishes. The process involves boiling water continuously in a wok or pan, creating steam and placing the food directly above the steam, which cooks the food. (Note: It is important to keep the food separate from the boiling water.)

Once you try steaming food you'll become an instant fan – ingredients are kept moist and vegetables retain a lot more of their nutrients, plus washing up is a doddle as most dishes are cooked in one pot.

Deep-frying

An important technique used in Chinese cooking, food is often prepared in advance with a coating of cornflour and egg before being plunged into hot oil. Although many believe this to be an unhealthy cooking method, the food seals very quickly on the outside, preventing further oil being absorbed. Food has a crisp outside texture while the inside remains very moist and juicy.

Shallow-frying or sautéing

This technique uses less oil than deep-frying; ingredients are first cooked on one side and then flipped over to cook the other side, ideal if using a shallow wok or frying pan. Shallow-fried or sautéed food is crispy on the outside and juicy on the inside.

Thickening

This technique is used to thicken sauces. Typically the thickening agent is a cornflour slurry (cornflour and a little water mixed, but potato starch can be used as well) which is poured into the dish at the end of the cooking process to thicken the sauce.

Banquet cooking

Whereas many of the recipes in this book give you the ingredient quantities to serve 2-4 people, if you are preparing a meal for the whole family or planning a large gathering, you can simply multiply the ingredients to increase the dishes to serve your extra guests. However, please be careful when increasing the salt, and start by first including the original recipe quantity and then adding to taste towards the end of cooking.

EQUIPMENT

Wok

A versatile round-bottomed cooking vessel originating from China. The use of the wok is very prevalent in south China where it's one of the most common cooking utensils.

A wok, in my opinion, is an essential piece of equipment in your kitchenware arsenal. This simple but uniquely designed pan can do pretty much anything. Buy a deep-sided wok and unlock a multitude of Chinese cooking techniques, including stir-frying, steaming, pan-frying, deep-frying, poaching, boiling, braising, searing, stewing and making soups.

Chinese cleaver

There are three basic types of cleaver used in the Chinese kitchen: the slicing cleaver, the cutting cleaver and the chopping cleaver. For beginners, a slicing cleaver is the perfect place to start. It's lightweight which makes it great for everyday use as it cuts everything from vegetables to boneless meat.

Chopping board

Walk into any Chinese home and you'll find a large, heavy, wooden chopping board. They are far less slippery than plastic chopping boards but either will work well. After using your chopping board, wash it in very hot water and use vinegar and lemon juice to sanitise it from time to time.

Ladle

A long-handled, bowl-shaped kitchen utensil which has been used for centuries by many Chinese cooks. It is the perfect tool for keeping the food moving around a very hot wok. If your wok is non-stick I do suggest you use a large wooden spoon instead because metallic cookware can damage the non-stick coating.

Chinese spatula

A long-handled spatula, shaped like a flat shovel, used to flip, toss and turn the ingredients when stir-frying in the wok.

Bamboo steamer

Developed over thousands of years in China, the bamboo steamer is a practical kitchen accessory you will use time and time again. It steams the food in tiers and is designed to sit snugly inside your wok.

Long chopsticks

Besides using chopsticks to eat with, the Chinese also like to use wooden chopsticks whilst cooking, especially when using the wok.

WOK CRAFT

'Good cooks never lack friends.'

Woks were originally designed to sit over a hole, hence their famous round bottoms, so trying to get an authentic wok to sit on top of a conventional cooker is nigh-on impossible without a wok ring. Wok rings (which can be bought in any Oriental supermarket) sit directly over the bars of a standard gas cooker and the wok nestles snugly on top.

In China woks are made from cast-iron or carbon-steel. They season beautifully (I'll go into seasoning in a second) and basically the more you use your wok, the more non-stick it becomes. Modern woks in the UK are generally made of stainless-steel, aluminium or metal clad with a non-stick coating. Stainless-steel and aluminium woks are difficult to season and food still sticks even at high temperatures so more oil is needed to stop this. Non-stick woks are, well, non-stick. When buying a non-stick wok, make sure it is hard-wearing and offers a lifetime guarantee.

'Seasoning' a wok is the term used for building thin layers of oil over the wok's surface to create a non-stick layer. Only cast-iron and carbon-steel woks can be seasoned successfully.

IMPORTANT

- Never use soap to wash your seasoned wok; rinse with hot water only.

- Always ensure your wok is completely dry before storage; the best way is to wipe dry and place over a low heat for 2 minutes until no water is visible. Allow to cool and then store.

- During your wok's infancy you'll damage the delicate seasoning layer you have just spent time developing if you use it for boiling or steaming, so use a different wok for these cooking techniques. Over time your wok will build up a strong layer and be more resilient.

THE SEASONING PROCESS

1 When you buy a new unseasoned wok, it will be coated in a layer of oil to protect the metal. This needs to be removed – wash in hot soapy water, scrub with a scourer and then rinse under hot water.

2 Thoroughly dry your wok by placing it over a low heat for 1–2 minutes and check to ensure all the water has evaporated.

3 Now heat your wok on high. After 30–40 seconds, check the temperature by carefully flicking a little water into the wok – little water beads should dance around and, after 1–2 seconds, evaporate.

4 Switch off the heat, add 2 tablespoons of sunflower or peanut oil and swirl the oil around so it coats the bottom and sides of your wok. If the oil smokes immediately, the wok is too hot. Allow to cool and start again.

5 Place your freshly oiled wok over a medium to low heat and add 6 spring onions (scallions), chopped into 4cm (1½in) pieces and 8 slices of ginger, each 3cm (1¼in) in length, skin on.

6 Stir-fry the aromatics for 15 minutes, smearing them around the inside of the wok, fully coating the entire surface. If the aromatics become too dry, add another tablespoon of oil. Your wok will begin to change to a yellow, blue, brown and maybe black colour and you'll notice a shine to the inside of the wok – this is the thin layer of oil building up.

7 Switch off the heat and allow your wok to cool. Once cooled, discard the spring onion and ginger and rinse out the wok with clean, warm water but DO NOT use soap/detergent.

8 Wipe the wok and place over a low heat for 2 minutes until completely dry, then remove from the heat and allow to cool. Your wok should now have a warm, subtle glow and is 'seasoned' or, in Cantonese, has 'wok hay' ('breath of a wok'). This final coating of oil will protect the seasoned layer that you will build up through use of your wok.

STARTERS & SOUPS

VEGETARIAN MINI SPRING ROLLS

In Chinese cuisine, spring rolls are savoury rolls with Chinese leaf and other vegetable fillings inside a thinly wrapped cylindrical pastry. They are usually eaten during the Spring Festival (Chinese New Year), hence the name.

20 MINUTES   **15 MINUTES**   **SERVES 4**

For the filling
1 tbsp groundnut oil
3 spring onions (scallions), sliced
2 garlic cloves, crushed
1 large carrot, peeled and finely shredded
½ Chinese leaf (Napa cabbage), shredded (1½ cups)
225g (8oz) tin water chestnuts, drained and roughly chopped
225g (8oz) tin bamboo shoots, drained and roughly chopped
50g (1 cup) beansprouts
1 tbsp light soy sauce
¼ tsp salt
¼ tsp white pepper
1 tsp sesame oil

20 spring roll wrappers (21.5cm/8½in square), defrosted in the packet before separating
2 tbsp cornflour (cornstarch) mixed with 1 tbsp beaten egg
groundnut oil for deep-frying
sweet chilli sauce, to serve

Heat a wok over a high heat until hot. Add the 1 tablespoon of the groundnut oil followed by the spring onions, garlic, carrot and Chinese leaves. Stir-fry for 2–3 minutes, until soft. Add the water chestnuts, bamboo shoots, beansprouts, soy sauce and salt and pepper. Stir-fry for a further minute, turn off heat and add the sesame oil. Transfer to a bowl and allow to cool.

Place a wrapper on a board with a corner pointing towards you, brush the edges with the cornflour and egg mixture. Spoon a good tablespoon of vegetable mixture into the corner of the wrapper. Fold the tip of the corner over the filling, creating an 8cm (3¼in) sausage shape, turn in the other two corners to enclose the filling and continue to roll. Repeat with the remaining wrappers and filling.

Pour enough oil into a wok so the spring rolls can float, heat to 160°C (325°F) and deep-fry the spring rolls in batches of four for 3–4 minutes, or until golden brown. Carefully lift from the oil and transfer to a wire rack or a plate lined with kitchen paper. Once all the spring rolls are cooked, serve hot with sweet chilli sauce for dipping.

Pictured on page 21, top

CRISPY SEAWEED

It's not seaweed at all! I'm not sure why Chinese seaweed is called seaweed when it's made from cabbage – all I know is how to make it and now I'm teaching you. In the restaurant we always served the seaweed with a sprinkle of dried fish powder (which just happens to taste lovely on top of vanilla ice cream!).

5 MINUTES   **10 MINUTES**   **SERVES 4**

300g (10½oz) Savoy cabbage, washed and thoroughly dried
groundnut oil for deep-frying
½ tsp sugar
½ tsp salt

Separate the cabbage into individual leaves, then remove the centre stem from each one. Place 4 de-stemmed leaves on top of one another and tightly roll into a tube, then using a very sharp knife slice very thin discs until you have a pile of finely chopped cabbage leaves. Repeat with the remaining leaves.

Heat enough oil in a wok so the cabbage can be deep-fried. Add about a quarter of the chopped cabbage, fry for about 1–2 minutes, until crispy. Remove the cabbage with a slotted spoon or Chinese sieve and dry on kitchen paper. Repeat with the remaining sliced cabbage.

Evenly sprinkle over salt and sugar. Toss well and transfer to a serving bowl. Serve straightaway.

Pictured on page 20, top

SESAME SEED PRAWN TOAST

This was one of the dishes that needed to be batch-made in the restaurant. It would start with peeling cases of king prawns in freezing cold water, turning your hands blue (brrrrrr), then we had to de-vein each prawn one-by-one and push the prawns through a mincer. Next we'd add the seasoning and cornflour and then beat the mixture for a good 20 minutes – this would stiffen it, making it more dense and springy. Finally we would spread the mixture onto pieces of white bread and then coat the prawn side in sesame seeds. It was an 'all-hands-on-deck' family affair. This recipe is much easier.

20 MINUTES   **5 MINUTES**   **SERVES 6-8**

280g (10oz) raw king prawns (tiger shrimp), peeled and de-veined
1 tbsp cornflour (cornstarch)
1 egg
½ tsp salt
4 slices of white bread
90g (⅔ cup) sesame seeds
groundnut oil for shallow frying

Put the prawns, cornflour, egg and salt into a food processor and blend to a paste.

Spread the paste onto one side of each slice of bread (don't skimp). Tip the sesame seeds on to a plate or chopping board, then press the bread, paste-side down, into the seeds. (Only seed the paste side!)

Heat 5–8cm (2–3in) of oil in a large pan or wok until hot but not smoking. Lower each slice of bread, one or two at a time (depending on the size of your wok), into the oil and fry for 30–50 seconds on each side, or until golden brown. Remove the toasts and transfer to a plate lined with kitchen paper to drain the excess oil. Remove the crusts and slice into triangles and serve (on average, allow 2–3 triangles per person).

The beauty of these toasts is that they can be prepared a day in advance and kept in the fridge. Once your guests start to arrive, fire up the cooker, fry the coated bread and you'll be serving tasty, home-made prawn toast in minutes.

Pictured on page 20, bottom

SATAY CHICKEN SKEWERS

This dish originates from Southeast Asia but has found its way onto most Chinese restaurant menus. Cook over an open BBQ and you'll be transported to the Far East with the smell of charcoal and smouldering spices.

5 MINUTES   **15 MINUTES**   **SERVES 4**

450g (1lb) chicken thighs or breast fillet, cut into 2cm (¾in) cubes
1½ tsp salt
¼ tsp white pepper
1 tbsp groundnut oil
240ml (1 cup) water
5 tbsp crunchy peanut butter
2 tbsp dark soy sauce
1 tbsp brown sugar
2 garlic cloves, crushed
1 tbsp lime juice

You'll need 24 wooden skewers (pre-soaked in water).

In a large bowl, combine the chicken with 1 teaspoon of the salt, the white pepper and the groundnut oil. Cover and transfer to the fridge to marinate for 2 hours. If you don't have time, don't worry; it's not essential.

Pour the water into a small saucepan and add the peanut butter, soy sauce, sugar, garlic and remaining salt, stirring to mix well, then bring to the boil. Once boiling, remove from the heat and add the lime juice.

Thread the marinated chicken onto the soaked skewers, making sure you have equal amounts on each skewer. Put 3 tablespoons of the peanut sauce to one side in a small bowl and brush the remainder of the sauce over the skewered chicken.

Heat a large frying pan or large griddle pan over a medium–high heat, then cook the chicken skewers for 2–2½ minutes per side. Ensure the chicken is cooked thoroughly before serving (slice one of the cubes in half to check there is no pink meat).

Serve the skewers with the remaining peanut sauce for dipping.

Pictured on page 21, bottom

SWEET CHINESE BBQ RIBS

Sticky, juicy and aromatic and a firm favourite for most carnivores, these ribs will tantalise your taste buds! They're so tender, the meat literally falls off the bones.

10 MINUTES   **1 HOUR**   **SERVES 4**

1kg (2lb 4oz) pork ribs, cut into
   8cm (3¼in) lengths
3 garlic cloves, finely chopped
5cm (2in) piece of fresh ginger,
   peeled and finely chopped
1 spring onion (scallion), halved
2 tbsp Chinese five spice
8 tbsp hoisin sauce
8 tbsp yellow bean sauce
50g (¼ cup) sugar
4 tbsp rice wine
2 tsp salt
1 litre (4¼ cups) chicken stock
2 tbsp cornflour (cornstarch)
   mixed with 4 tbsp water
2 tbsp groundnut oil
3 tbsp runny honey (optional)

In a large saucepan with a lid, place the ribs and all of the ingredients except the stock, cornflour slurry, oil and honey, and massage them into the meat. Now add enough stock so the ribs are almost completely submerged under the liquid. Bring the pan to a boil, turn down to a simmer and place the lid on the pan. Cook on low for 30 minutes (keep an eye on the sauce and add more stock if necessary). Remove the ribs from the sauce and place on a wire rack set over a bowl to drain.

Preheat the oven to 200°C (400°F). Strain the remainder of the sauce through a sieve into a clean saucepan and bring back to a boil. Slowly add the cornflour slurry while stirring to thicken the sauce to the desired consistency, ideally so that the sauce coats the back of a spoon. Turn off the heat and set to one side.

Arrange the ribs on a baking tray, lightly brush with the oil and place in the hot oven for 10 minutes (make sure they do not burn). Remove from the oven and brush the ribs with the thickened BBQ sauce or, if you like, some honey, and put back into the oven for another 5 minutes. Serve on a large plate with the remainder of the BBQ sauce.

Tip
If you're looking to achieve the 'red glow' that you see on restaurant ribs, you can always add a dash of red food colouring to the sauce mixture at the start of the cooking process.

CRISPY AROMATIC DUCK WITH HOISIN SAUCE AND PANCAKES

Everyone, and I do mean everyone, LOVES this dish; it's the perfect sharing plate to be enjoyed with friends and family.

10 MINUTES   **1-2 HOURS**   **SERVES 4-6**   **2 HOURS +**

4 spring onions (scallions), halved
a thumb-sized piece of fresh
   unpeeled ginger, sliced
1 litre (4¼ cups) chicken stock
120ml (½ cup) rice wine
120ml (½ cup) dark soy sauce
100g (½ cup) demerara sugar
1½ tbsp Chinese five spice
2 star anise
1 tsp cloves
3 cinnamon sticks
½ tbsp salt
4 duck legs (or you can use a whole
   duck cut into quarters)

To assemble
1 pack of Chinese pancakes
   (average 10 pancakes per pack)
2 spring onions (scallions), cut into
   matchsticks
1 cucumber, cut into matchsticks
60ml (¼ cup) hoisin sauce

Put the spring onions, ginger, stock, rice wine, soy sauce, sugar, spices and salt into a large, lidded saucepan and stir well to combine. Add the duck legs and massage the marinade into the skin. Pop the lid on, put the pan in the fridge and leave to marinate for at least 2 hours or ideally overnight.

At the end of the marinating time, take the lid off the pan and set it over a high heat, bring to the boil, then turn down to a simmer. Cover and cook for 1-2 hours, keeping an eye on the liquid to ensure it doesn't boil dry – add water if needed. Remove the duck legs from the liquid and place on a wire rack to cool. Preheat the oven to 220°C (425°F).

Arrange the duck legs on a baking tray and cook in the oven for around 15–20 minutes, or until the skin has turned lovely and crispy.

Towards the end of the duck's cooking time, steam the pancakes for 6 minutes (or according to the packet instructions).

Remove the duck from the oven and shred the meat from the bones using two forks. Serve straight away with the warm pancakes, spring onions, cucumber and hoisin sauce and let everyone fill and roll their own pancakes.

CLASSIC PANCAKE ROLLS

Chinese pancake rolls are very popular in Chinese fish & chip shops. We used to sell dozens of them in my parents' chippy. Five times bigger than the mini spring rolls served in Cantonese restaurants, these large cylindrical parcels are packed full of beansprouts and ooze as you bite into them.

20 MINUTES   **15 MINUTES**   **SERVES 4-8**

For the filling
1 tbsp groundnut oil
2 spring onions (scallions), sliced
2 garlic cloves, crushed
6cm (2½in) piece of fresh ginger, peeled and finely chopped
1 large carrot, peeled and finely shredded
40g (¼ cup) tinned water chestnuts, roughly chopped
30g (¼ cup) tinned bamboo shoots, roughly chopped
6 baby corn cobs, cut into quarters lengthways
150g (3 cups) beansprouts
40g (1½oz) shredded char siu pork (see page 100) (or purchase from a Chinese supermarket)
40g (1½oz) cooked chicken, shredded
30g (1oz) cooked and peeled prawns (shrimp)
1 tbsp light soy sauce
½ tsp salt
¼ tsp white pepper
½ tbsp dark soy sauce
1 tsp sesame oil

8 spring roll wrappers (21.5cm/ 8½in square), defrosted in the packet before separating
2 tbsp cornflour (cornstarch)
1 egg, beaten
groundnut oil for deep-frying

Heat a wok over high heat until hot. Add the 1 tablespoon of oil, followed by the spring onions, garlic, ginger and carrot. Stir-fry for 2–3 minutes until soft. Add the water chestnuts, bamboo shoots, baby corn, beansprouts, pork, chicken, shrimps, light soy sauce, salt and pepper and stir-fry for a further minute. Add the dark soy and mix thoroughly, then turn off the heat and add the sesame oil. Transfer to a bowl and leave the filling to cool.

In a small bowl, mix the cornflour with a tablespoon of the beaten egg. Place a wrapper on a board with a corner pointing towards you and brush the edges with the cornflour and egg mixture. Spoon 2–3 generous tablespoons of filling into the centre of the wrapper, fold the corner over the filling, turn in the side corners to enclose and create a large fat sausage shape, then roll towards the final corner. Brush with the remaining beaten egg and seal. Repeat with remaining wrappers and filling.

Pour enough oil into a wok so the pancake rolls can float, heat to 160°C (325°F) and deep-fry the spring rolls in batches of two for 5–6 minutes, or until golden brown. Remove to a wire rack or a plate lined with kitchen paper. Once all of the pancake rolls are cooked, serve hot.

FIVE SPICE RIBS

To all you carnivores out there, this one's for you! Sink your teeth into a lip-smackingly sweet sticky rib and don't forget your bib. It's gonna get messy!

40 MINUTES   **1 HOUR**   **SERVES 4**   **30 MINS**

1kg (2lb 4oz) pork ribs, cut into 8cm (3¼in) lengths
groundnut oil for deep-frying
2 garlic cloves, crushed
1½ tbsp Chinese five spice
2 spring onions (scallions), finely chopped
3 tbsp sugar
3 tbsp Chinese rice wine
240ml (1 cup) chicken stock
1½ tbsp light soy sauce
1 tbsp grated orange zest
120ml (½ cup) rice vinegar

For the marinade
2 tbsp Chinese rice wine
1 tbsp light soy sauce
½ tbsp dark soy sauce
1 tbsp rice vinegar
2 tsp sesame oil
1 tbsp cornflour (cornstarch)

Mix the marinade ingredients together in a large bowl. Add the ribs and massage the marinade into the meat. Leave to marinate for at least 30 minutes, then remove the ribs from the marinade and drain on a wire rack for 10 minutes.

Heat enough oil in a large wok or saucepan to deep-fry the ribs. Once the oil has reached 170°C (340°F), carefully and slowly fry the ribs in batches of 5, until they have browned – this will take around 10 minutes. Remove from the oil and drain on a wire rack.

In a large pan, put the garlic, five spice, spring onions, sugar, rice wine, chicken stock, soy sauce, orange zest and rice vinegar and bring to the boil. Add the deep-fried ribs and turn the heat to very low. Cover the pan and allow the ribs to blip away for 40 minutes, stirring occasionally (add more water if the sauce becomes too dry).

Remove the lid, turn up the heat and reduce the sauce (taking care not to burn anything) until it clings to the ribs. Transfer to a serving plate and enjoy.

To make your own five spice powder:
Place a wok over a medium–high heat, add 2 crumbled star anise, 1 teaspoon Sichuan peppercorns, 2½ teaspoons fennel seeds, 8 whole cloves and 1 cinnamon stick, crumbled, and toast, being careful not to burn them. Once the air is filled with the heavy scent of aromatics pour the spices onto a plate to cool. When cool, grind the toasted spices in a grinder or mortar and pestle until you have a fine powder. Store in an airtight jar and use within a month.

DEEP-FRIED
CRISPY WONTONS

We Chinese have a serious love affair with these little crispy pockets filled with succulent, juicy yumminess. Deep-fried, every mouthful is sheer perfection – crispy, juicy, aromatic, salty and sweet, all in one mouthful!

20 MINUTES   **15 MINUTES**   **SERVES 6**

¼ tsp salt
½ medium Chinese cabbage, finely chopped (you want about 225g/8oz)
225g (8oz) minced pork
1 tsp light soy sauce
¼ tsp freshly ground black pepper
1 tsp cornflour (cornstarch)
1 tsp Chinese rice wine (optional)
½ tsp sesame oil
2 spring onions (scallions), finely chopped
110g (4oz) tinned water chestnuts, finely chopped
½ tsp grated fresh ginger
3–4 shiitake or portobello mushrooms, finely diced
1 pack of wonton wrappers
1 egg, beaten
groundnut oil for deep-frying
sweet chilli sauce, to serve

Sprinkle the salt over the chopped cabbage in a large bowl, stir to combine and set aside.

In a separate large bowl, mix the pork with the soy sauce, ground pepper, cornflour, rice wine (if using) and sesame oil. Add the spring onions, water chestnuts, ginger and mushrooms and mix well to combine. You might need to use your hands for this (wash your hands before and afterwards).

Take handfuls of the cabbage and squeeze over the sink to remove excess water, then add to the bowl with the rest of the filling ingredients. Mix together well. If the mixture is too wet, add a little more cornflour to thicken.

Angle a wonton wrapper so that it faces you like a diamond. Use your fingertips or a teaspoon to spread a thin layer of egg wash along the top two edges of the wrapper. Place ¼ teaspoon of filling in the centre of the wrapper, fold the bottom tip to the top tip to form a triangle, pinch along the edge of the filling to seal the wonton and squeeze out the air.

Heat a wok or deep-sided saucepan over a medium heat with enough oil so the wontons can float. When the oil reaches 170°C (340°F), carefully drop the wontons into the oil in batches of five. Fry for 4–5 minutes, turning regularly to ensure even cooking and browning. Once cooked, lift from the oil using a slotted spoon or a Chinese sieve and drain the wontons on a wire rack while you cook the rest. Arrange on a plate and serve with your favourite sweet chilli sauce.

SWEET CHILLI CRISPY WINGS

Double-fried, super-crunchy, spicy and juicy wings... This recipe does take a little longer to cook, but to get the crispy coating on the wing you have to double-fry. I guarantee that once you try this dish, it will become the one you pull out of the bag to wow your friends and family – it really is that good!

10 MINUTES   **30 MINUTES**   **SERVES 4**

1.6kg (3lb 8oz) chicken wings
½ tsp salt
½ tsp freshly ground black pepper
1 tsp grated fresh ginger
125g (1 cup) cornflour (cornstarch)
vegetable oil for frying
4 garlic cloves, crushed
3 large, dried red chillies, de-seeded and cut into quarters
60ml (¼ cup) light soy sauce
120ml (½ cup) runny honey
1 tbsp rice wine vinegar
1 tbsp palm sugar
1 tbsp sesame seeds, toasted

Pat the chicken wings with kitchen paper to make sure they are absolutely dry. Cut the tips off each wing and then cut each wing in half.

Put the chicken into a large bowl and mix with the salt, pepper and ginger. Add the cornflour to a separate large bowl, then thoroughly coat each chicken wing, gently squeezing to make sure the flour is sticking. Put the coated wings on a plate and set aside.

Heat a large non-stick wok over a medium to high heat. Add 1–2 tablespoons of oil, then fry the garlic and chillies for 30 seconds, taking care not to burn the garlic. Add the soy sauce, honey and vinegar, mix well and simmer for a couple of minutes. Add the palm sugar and stir until fully dissolved. Remove from the heat and set aside.

Put enough vegetable oil in a large saucepan to be deep enough to deep-fry the wings, and heat to 170°C (340°F). Gently fry the wings in batches of five, cooking for 8–10 minutes depending on the thickness of each wing piece. Turn the wings frequently to ensure even cooking. Remove wings and drain on a wire rack. Continue until all the wings are fried.

Once all the wings are cooked and slightly cooled, reheat the oil (to the same temperature) and fry the wings again for another 12 minutes, until golden brown and crispy, remembering to turn the wings frequently. Remove and drain on a wire rack and repeat with the rest of the wings.

When all the chicken has been double-fried, reheat the sauce in the wok, add the wings and mix well to coat. Transfer to a serving plate, sprinkle with toasted sesame seeds and serve straightaway.

CHICKEN YUK SUNG

Finely diced chicken stir-fried with classic Chinese aromatics, served in crisp Iceberg lettuce leaves with crispy vermicelli (optional but highly recommended for added texture!) – deliciously light and tasty, creating the perfect mouthful.

10 MINUTES　　**15 MINUTES**　　**SERVES 2-4**

2 tbsp groundnut oil
2 garlic cloves, finely chopped
3cm (1¼in) piece of fresh ginger, peeled and finely sliced
3 spring onions (scallions), finely sliced
500g (1lb 2oz) chicken, finely chopped
1½ tbsp dark soy sauce
3 tbsp oyster sauce
1 tbsp rice wine
1 tbsp granulated sugar
1 medium onion, finely chopped
1 large carrot, finely chopped
225g (8oz) tin of water chestnuts, drained and finely chopped
1 tbsp sesame oil
1 Iceberg lettuce, separated into individual leaves, washed and dried

For the vermicelli (optional)
60ml (¼ cup) vegetable oil for frying
a handful of dried rice vermicelli noodles

Gently heat 1 tablespoon of the groundnut oil in a wok. Add the garlic, ginger and spring onions and fry until the ginger and garlic are aromatic, about 30 seconds. Add the chicken and cook for about 3-5 minutes, until browned. Scrape everything into a bowl and set aside.

In a small bowl, mix the soy sauce, oyster sauce, rice wine and sugar.

Heat the remaining groundnut oil in the wok over a medium heat, add the onion, carrot and water chestnuts and cook for 2-3 minutes, or until softened and browned. Add the soy sauce mixture and mix in well. Return the chicken back into the wok and cook over a medium heat for about 2-3 minutes, until the sauce has reduced – the mixture should be quite dry. Add the sesame oil and mix well.

If you're making the crispy vermicelli garnish, heat the vegetable oil in a frying pan over a medium heat and add the noodles – they will puff up FAST! Drain on kitchen paper ready for serving.

To serve, spoon some of the yuk sung and some fried vermicelli into a lettuce leaf, wrap and eat!

Tip
The best way to separate lettuce leaves while keeping them intact is to hold the lettuce under a gently running cold tap – as the leaves fill with water they peel (intact) away from the lettuce.

CHICKEN AND SWEETCORN SOUP

A big bowl of soup is sometimes all you really need. This recipe is quick, tasty and completely hassle-free. I'm sure once you give it a go it'll become your go-to dish when all you really want is a big bowl of satisfaction.

5 MINUTES   **8 MINUTES**   **SERVES 4**

800ml (3⅓ cups) chicken or vegetable stock
420g (15oz) tin of creamed corn
170g (6oz) cooked chicken, shredded
¼ tsp white pepper
salt, to taste
30g (¼ cup) peas
2 tbsp cornflour (cornstarch) mixed with 4 tbsp water
1 egg, beaten
1 tsp sesame oil

In a non-stick wok or medium-sized saucepan, combine the stock, creamed corn and chicken and bring to the boil. Reduce the heat and season with the pepper and add salt to taste, then add the peas and bring back to the boil.

Stir the cornflour and water slurry and, while the soup is boiling, pour it in slowly, stirring the soup constantly until you have the desired consistency. Turn the heat down to low, slowly pour in the beaten egg, again stirring the soup at the same time. Switch off the heat, add the sesame oil, give it a quick stir and serve hot.

PEKING HOT AND SOUR SOUP

Developed in the Sichuan province of China, this soup is both spicy and sour. As soups go, this one is a must as it combines most of the elements you need to create a perfect mouthful: crunchy vegetables, succulent meats, a sharp twang from the vinegar and the subtle warmth of chilli.

5 MINUTES   **8 MINUTES**   **SERVES 4**

½ tbsp dark soy sauce
1 tbsp light soy sauce
6 tbsp rice vinegar
2 dried chillies, finely chopped
40g (1½oz) char siu pork (see page 100 or purchase from a Chinese supermarket), cut into matchsticks
30g (¼ cup) cooked and peeled prawns (shrimp)
15g (½oz) dried wood ear mushrooms, rehydrated in hot water, drained and cut into matchsticks
30g (1oz) firm tofu, cut into 1cm (½in) cubes
30g (1oz) tinned bamboo shoots, cut into matchsticks
½ medium carrot, cut into matchsticks
30g (¼ cup) peas
1.8 litres (7½ cups) chicken stock
½ tsp white pepper
1½ tsp salt
2 tsp sugar
4 tbsp tomato ketchup
1 tsp tomato purée
6 tbsp cornflour (cornstarch) mixed with 12 tbsp water
2 eggs, beaten
½ tbsp sesame oil

Put all of the ingredients, apart from the cornflour mixture, sesame oil and eggs, into a large wok or saucepan. Slowly bring to the boil, then lower the heat and let the soup simmer for 3 minutes.

Give the cornflour mix a good stir, turn the heat up to medium and slowly add the cornflour to the soup, stirring as you go, until you reach the desired consistency. Turn off the heat and slowly pour in the beaten eggs, stirring as you pour.

Finally, add the sesame oil and serve.

CHICKEN NOODLE SOUP

Food for the body is not enough – there must also be food for the soul!

15 MINUTES   **10 MINUTES**   **SERVES 4**

1 nest of dried egg noodles
3cm (1¼in) piece of fresh ginger,
  peeled and thinly sliced
1 tbsp light soy sauce
800ml (3⅓ cups) chicken stock
200g (7oz) chicken breast fillet,
  thinly sliced
½ tsp white pepper
1 tsp salt
1 tsp sesame oil
1 spring onion (scallion), finely sliced,
  to garnish

Boil a saucepan of water and cook the noodles for around 3 minutes, or until soft, then drain. Divide the noodles between 4 serving bowls.

Add the remaining ingredients, except the sesame oil and spring onions, to a saucepan, bring to the boil, turn the heat down and simmer for 3 minutes. Remove from the heat and add the sesame oil. Pour the soup evenly over the noodles and garnish with spring onions.

CHICKEN AND MUSHROOM SOUP

Super quick to make, this soup is the perfect winter warmer.

---

15 MINUTES   **10 MINUTES**   **SERVES 2**

500ml (generous 2 cups) chicken stock

200g (7oz) chicken breast fillet, thinly sliced

1 tbsp light soy sauce

1 tbsp oyster sauce

6 mushrooms, thinly sliced

1 spring onion (scallion), finely sliced

½ tsp white pepper

1 tsp salt

1 tsp sesame oil

Heat the stock in a wok or saucepan over a medium heat. Add the sliced chicken and bring to a boil, then add the soy sauce, oyster sauce, mushrooms, half the chopped spring onion, the pepper and salt. Stir well and simmer for 3 minutes.

Remove from the heat, stir in the sesame oil and serve in bowls, garnished with remaining spring onions.

WONTON SOUP

If one dish summed up our family's food history, this would be the dish. As a teen, Dad worked in a wonton bar in Sha-Tau-Kok, in the New Territories of Hong Kong, which borders China. This is where Dad first learnt his trade and skill, a skill that would be later passed to me. Won-ton translated literally means 'swallow cloud' because after the wontons have been cooked, the dumplings float in the soup, resembling small clouds.

15 MINUTES   **10 MINUTES**   **SERVES 4**

For the wontons
100g (3½oz) minced pork
100g (3½oz) raw king prawns (tiger shrimp), peeled, de-veined and finely chopped
1cm (½in) piece of fresh ginger, finely chopped
½ tbsp light soy sauce
1½ tsp rice vinegar
¼ tsp salt
¼ tsp white pepper
1 tsp sesame oil
1–2 tsp cornflour (cornstarch), only if mixture is too wet
1 egg
24 wonton wrappers

For the soup
3cm (1¼in) piece of fresh ginger, peeled and thinly sliced
1 tbsp soy sauce
800ml (3⅓ cups) chicken stock
½ tsp white pepper
1 tsp salt

To serve
1 spring onion (scallion), finely sliced
1 tsp sesame oil

First make the wontons. In a large mixing bowl, combine the minced pork, chopped prawns, ginger, soy sauce, vinegar, salt, pepper and sesame oil and thoroughly mix all of the ingredients together. The filling should be slightly sticky but if it seems too wet, mix in 1–2 teaspoons of cornflour to thicken it.

Crack the egg into a bowl and beat with a fork.

Place a wonton wrapper on a chopping board and position it so that it faces you like a diamond. With your fingertips or a spoon, spread a thin layer of the egg wash along the top two edges of the wrapper. Place a quarter of a teaspoon of filling in the centre of the wrapper, fold the bottom tip to the top tip to form a triangle and pinch along the edge of the filling to seal the wonton, squeezing out the air. Wet the tip of one of the long ends of the triangle tips and fold into the centre, then fold the other tip into the centre and join the two together. Repeat until you've filled all the wrappers and used up the filling.

Now make the soup. Put all the soup ingredients into a large saucepan and bring to the boil, then turn down the heat to simmer for 5-8 minutes.

Fill another large saucepan with water and bring to the boil. Carefully drop the wontons into the boiling water and cook for 3–4 minutes. Once the wontons float to the surface they should be cooked thoroughly but please check before eating. There should be no pink meat.

Divide the wontons between four soup bowls and sprinkle with chopped spring onions and a drizzle of sesame oil. Pour over the soup and serve.

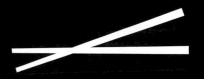

HONEY AND LEMON CHICKEN

This was a firm favourite in my dad's Cantonese restaurant –
delicate, battered crispy chicken served on a bed of pineapple
and drenched in a sweet yet tangy lemon sauce.

10 MINUTES   **10 MINUTES**   **SERVES 2**

For the chicken
groundnut oil for deep-frying
2 large chicken breast fillets
½ tsp salt
80g (⅔ cup) cornflour (cornstarch)
1 egg

For the honey and lemon sauce
120ml (½ cup) lemon cordial
3 tbsp runny honey
1 tbsp custard powder
200g (7oz) drained tinned pineapple
  chunks
½ lemon, cut into slices, to garnish

First, start to make the sauce. Pour the cordial and honey into a wok
and add the custard powder. Stir over a medium heat until the sauce
starts to boil. Lower the heat and stir continuously, until you reach the
desired consistency. Remove from the heat and set to one side.

Heat a large saucepan or wok over a medium to high heat and fill
with enough oil so it's deep enough for the chicken to float. Heat to
170°C (345°F).

Meanwhile, butterfly each chicken breast (slice through the breast
horizontally but not all the way through, then open it out so it
resembles a butterfly). Season with the salt. Tip the cornflour onto
a large plate, break the egg into a wide shallow bowl and beat.
Coat the chicken on the cornflour, brushing off any excess, then
dip the floured chicken into the beaten egg. Coat the chicken with
cornflour for a second time, brushing off excess flour.

Carefully lower the chicken into the hot oil and deep-fry for 6–8
minutes, or until the chicken is golden brown, crispy and cooked all
the way through. If you have a food probe thermometer, the internal
temperature of the chicken should be at least 78°C (175°F). Transfer
to a wire rack to drain or onto a plate lined with kitchen paper.

Reheat the sauce and arrange the pineapple on a serving plate.
Slice the chicken into bite-sized pieces, place on top of the pineapple
and garnish with the sliced lemon. Pour the sauce over the top and
serve straightaway.

CHICKEN WITH SWEET GINGER AND PINEAPPLE

'The Chinese do not draw any distinction between food and medicine.' *The Importance of Living*, Lin Yutang

Ginger has many medicinal uses and is used in its many forms – fresh, dried, preserved, powdered, ground and candied – in hundreds of Chinese recipes.

Way back when, in my parents' Chinese Restaurant, there were jars and jars of sweet ginger on the storeroom shelves ready to prepare this sweetly fragrant and aromatic dish.

---

10 MINUTES   **10 MINUTES**   **SERVES 2**

1 tbsp groundnut oil
300g (10½oz) chicken breast fillet, cut into thin slices
1 garlic clove, finely chopped
1 onion, roughly chopped
1 carrot, cut into thin thumb-sized slices (slice the carrot diagonally)
8 slices of Chinese sweet pickled ginger
100g (3½oz) drained tinned pineapple chunks
1 tbsp rice vinegar
½ tsp salt
1 tbsp granulated sugar
120ml (½ cup) chicken stock
1 tbsp tomato ketchup
1 tsp sesame oil
1 tbsp cornflour (cornstarch) mixed with 2 tbsp water

Heat the groundnut oil in a wok over a medium heat. Add the chicken and stir-fry for 2–3 minutes, then add the garlic and stir-fry for a further 15 seconds, followed by the onion and carrot. Stir-fry for a further minute before adding the sweet ginger and pineapple, stirring to combine well.

Add the vinegar, salt, sugar, stock and ketchup, bring to the boil then reduce the heat and simmer for 1 minute. Slowly add the cornflour mixture, stirring the sauce continuously. Remove from the heat, stir in the sesame oil and serve straightaway with a bowl of steaming Egg Fried Rice (see page 129).

CHICKEN AND MUSHROOMS

This dish will work with any type of edible mushroom you can get your hands on. Experiment – the kitchen is your playground!

5 MINUTES   **7 MINUTES**   **SERVES 2**

200g (7oz) portobello mushrooms
1 tbsp groundnut oil
3 garlic cloves, crushed
½ tsp finely chopped fresh ginger
2 chicken breast fillets, thinly sliced
2 tbsp oyster sauce
1 tbsp dark soy sauce
¼ tsp salt
¼ tsp white pepper
1 tsp granulated sugar
80ml (⅓ cup) chicken stock
1 tbsp cornflour (cornstarch) mixed
    with 2 tbsp water
1 tsp sesame oil

Cut the mushrooms into bite-sized pieces if necessary. Place a wok over a medium–high heat, add the groundnut oil, garlic and ginger and fry for about 30 seconds, until fragrant. Add the chicken and stir-fry for 2 minutes, then add the mushrooms and stir-fry for a further minute.

Add the oyster sauce, soy sauce, salt, white pepper, sugar and chicken stock and mix well. Bring the sauce to the boil and allow to reduce by a third – this will take about 2 minutes. Pour in the cornflour mixture to thicken the sauce, stirring the entire time, remove from the heat and add the sesame oil. Transfer to a serving dish and enjoy with rice.

CHICKEN AND CASHEW NUTS

When cooking Chinese food, it's always important to think about the flavours and textures of the ingredients. Juicy chicken combined with succulent baby corn and salty, crunchy cashew nuts come together beautifully in this dish.

5 MINUTES   **7 MINUTES**   **SERVES 2**

1 tbsp groundnut oil

3 garlic cloves, crushed

½ tsp finely chopped fresh ginger

2 chicken breast fillets, sliced

1 onion, roughly chopped

1 carrot, finely diced

40g (¼ cup) tinned water chestnuts, sliced into bite-sized discs

30g (¼ cup) tinned bamboo shoots

3 baby corn cobs, cut into bite-sized pieces

2 tbsp oyster sauce

1 tbsp dark soy sauce

80ml (⅓ cup) chicken stock

¼ tsp salt

¼ tsp white pepper

1 tbsp cornflour (cornstarch) mixed with 2 tbsp water

30g (1oz) salted, roasted cashew nuts

1 tsp sesame oil

Place a wok over a medium–high heat, add the groundnut oil, garlic and ginger and fry for about 30 seconds, until fragrant. Add the chicken and stir-fry for 2 minutes. Add the onion, carrot, water chestnuts, bamboo shoots and baby corn and stir-fry for a further 2 minutes. Spoon in the oyster sauce and soy sauce, pour in the stock and add the salt and pepper. Stir well, bring to the boil and then turn down to simmer for 2 minutes.

Pour in the cornflour mixture to thicken the sauce, stirring as you do, then remove from the heat, add the cashew nuts and sesame oil and mix well. Transfer to a serving dish and enjoy.

CHICKEN AND STRAW MUSHROOMS

Straw mushrooms are grown on rice straw beds in Southeast Asia and are picked when they are still immature during the button phase of their growing cycle. As a child I remember thinking they looked like little sheep's eyes peeping at me from the plate!

5 MINUTES   **7 MINUTES**   **SERVES 2**

1 tbsp groundnut oil
3 garlic cloves, crushed
2 chicken breast fillets, thinly sliced
1 onion, roughly chopped
1 carrot, finely diced
30g (¼ cup) tinned bamboo shoots
130g (1 cup) tinned straw
  mushrooms, chopped in
  half lengthways
2 tbsp oyster sauce
1 tbsp light soy sauce
½ tbsp dark soy sauce
1 tsp salt
½ tsp white pepper
80ml (⅓ cup) chicken stock
1 tbsp cornflour (cornstarch) mixed
  with 2 tbsp water
1 tsp sesame oil

Place a wok over a medium–high heat, add the groundnut oil and garlic and fry for about 15 seconds, until fragrant. Add the chicken and stir-fry for 2 minutes, then add the onion and carrot and stir-fry for a further 2 minutes. Add the bamboo shoots, mushrooms, oyster and soy sauces, salt and pepper. Pour in the stock, bring to the boil and then turn down to simmer for 2 minutes.

Pour in the cornflour mixture to thicken the sauce, stirring as you do, then remove from the heat, stir in the sesame oil and serve.

CHICKEN AND PINEAPPLE

The subtle taste of aromatic garlic against the sweet pineapple creates a taste explosion, and combined with a twang from the tomato ketchup, this dish will have you drooling for more.

5 MINUTES   **7 MINUTES**   **SERVES 2**

1 tbsp groundnut oil

1 garlic clove, crushed

2 chicken breast fillets, thinly sliced

1 onion, chopped

1 carrot, thinly cut into thumb-sized slices (cut the carrot diagonally)

1 green (bell) pepper, de-seeded and cut into 3cm (1¼in) cubes

2 tbsp rice vinegar

125g (1 cup) drained tinned pineapple chunks

½ tsp salt

1 tbsp granulated sugar

1 tbsp tomato ketchup

1 tsp tomato purée

120ml (½ cup) chicken stock

1 tbsp cornflour (cornstarch) mixed with 2 tbsp water

1 tsp sesame oil

Place a wok over a medium–high heat, add the groundnut oil and garlic and fry for about 15 seconds, until fragrant. Add the chicken and stir-fry for 2 minutes. Add the onion, carrot and pepper and stir-fry for a further 2 minutes.

Add the vinegar, pineapple, salt, sugar, tomato ketchup and purée and stock, bring to the boil and then turn down the heat to simmer for 2 minutes.

Pour in the cornflour mixture to thicken the sauce, stirring as you go, then remove from the heat, stir in the sesame oil and mix well. Transfer to a serving dish and enjoy.

SPICY HOI SIN CHICKEN

Sweet, rich, tangy and aromatic, this is the perfect sauce to smother your chicken in. (NB If your cashew nuts are salted, rinse them in cold water and dry with kitchen paper.)

5 MINUTES **7 MINUTES** **SERVES 2**

1 tbsp groundnut oil
4 garlic cloves, crushed
1 tsp finely chopped fresh ginger
2 chicken breast fillets, sliced
1 onion, roughly chopped
1 carrot, finely diced
40g (¼ cup) tinned water chestnuts, sliced into bite-sized discs
30g (¼ cup) tinned bamboo shoots
1 tbsp rice vinegar
1 tbsp dark soy sauce
120ml (½ cup) hoisin sauce
½ tsp dried chilli flakes
1 tsp sesame oil
30g (¼ cup) unsalted, roasted cashew nuts

Place a wok over a medium–high heat and add the groundnut oil, garlic and ginger and fry for about 15 seconds, until fragrant. Add the chicken and stir-fry for 2 minutes, then add the onion, carrot, water chestnuts and bamboo shoots and stir-fry for a further 2 minutes. Lower the heat to medium and add the vinegar, soy sauce, hoisin sauce and chilli flakes and stir-fry for a further 2–3 minutes.

Remove from the heat, add the sesame oil and cashew nuts and mix well. Transfer to a serving dish and enjoy.

SWEET AND SOUR CHICKEN BALLS

Friday nights just wouldn't be the same without these balls of chicken loveliness.

---

10 MINUTES   **15 MINUTES**   **SERVES 4**

125g (1 cup) plain (all-purpose) flour

2 tsp baking powder (soda)

1 tsp salt

2 eggs

160ml (⅔ cup) semi-skimmed milk

1 tbsp groundnut oil, plus enough for deep-frying

4 chicken breast fillets, cut into 3cm (1¼in) cubes

For the sweet and sour sauce

240ml (1 cup) orange juice

3 tbsp sugar

1 tbsp tomato purée

1 tbsp tomato ketchup

3 tbsp white wine vinegar

3 tbsp cornflour (cornstarch) mixed with 6 tbsp water

First make the sauce – put all the ingredients, apart from the cornflour mixture, into a large saucepan over a medium heat. Bring to the boil and then simmer for 5 minutes. Slowly pour the cornflour mixture into the sauce a little at a time, stirring continuously, until you have the desired consistency, then take off the heat and set to one side.

Mix the flour, baking powder and salt in a large bowl. In a separate bowl, beat the eggs, milk and the 1 tablespoon of oil together. Pour the wet mixture into the flour and mix well to create a smooth paste. Add the chicken and mix, making sure each piece is thoroughly coated.

Heat oil to 170°C (345°F) in a deep-sided saucepan or wok, ensuring you have enough oil in the wok so that the chicken will fry without touching the bottom. Carefully lower the chicken into the oil one piece at a time and fry in batches of 5 pieces for about 5–6 minutes, until golden brown and cooked thoroughly. If you have a food probe thermometer the internal temperature should reach 78°C (175°F). Remove the chicken from the oil and drain on a wire rack or on a plate lined with kitchen paper. Repeat until you've fried all the chicken, then serve with the sweet and sour dipping sauce.

CHINESE CHICKEN CURRY

Introduced into China by the Cantonese from Malaysia, this signature sauce is often also served with fish balls and beef brisket.

---

5 MINUTES   **25 MINUTES**   **SERVES 2**

1 tbsp groundnut oil
2 chicken breast fillets, sliced into thin strips
1 onion, roughly chopped
4 button mushrooms, sliced
¼ tsp salt
¼ tsp sugar
40g (¼ cup) peas

For the curry sauce
1 tbsp groundnut oil
2 onions, sliced into strips
5 garlic cloves, crushed
2 carrots, sliced into small discs
2 tbsp plain (all-purpose) flour
4 tsp curry powder (use your favourite: mild, medium or hot)
600ml (2½ cups) chicken stock
2 tsp honey
4 tsp light soy sauce
1 bay leaf
1 tsp garam masala

First, make the curry sauce: heat the oil in a wok or non-stick saucepan, add the onion and garlic and cook until softened. Stir in the carrots and cook over a low heat for 10–12 minutes.

Add the flour and curry powder and cook for 1 minute. Gradually stir in the stock until combined, then add the honey, soy sauce and bay leaf. Slowly bring to the boil, then reduce the heat and simmer for 15 minutes or until the sauce thickens but is still a pouring consistency. Stir in the garam masala, then strain the curry sauce through a sieve and set to one side.

Heat the oil in a wok over a medium heat and, when hot, add the chicken and stir-fry for 2 minutes. Add the onion and mushrooms and fry for a further 2–3 minutes, ensuring the chicken is cooked thoroughly. Now add the salt and sugar, mix well, then pour in the strained curry sauce and add the peas. Bring to the boil, then reduce the heat to simmer for 3 minutes, allowing the curry sauce to thicken again. If the curry sauce is too thick, add a splash of water to loosen it. Serve with Perfect Steamed Rice (see page 128).

SHREDDED CRISPY CHICKEN WITH BLACK PEPPER AND SALT

'People who love to eat are always the best people.' Julia Child

This dish is truly a taste sensation, from the crispy crust wrapped around the juicy strips of chicken, to the speckled heat of black pepper and salty, five spice sauce.

10 MINUTES   **10 MINUTES**   **SERVES 2**

½ tbsp salt
½ tbsp Chinese five spice
½ tbsp freshly ground black pepper
1 tbsp groundnut oil, plus extrta for deep-frying
2 chicken breast fillets, cut into thin strips
50g (½ cup) cornflour (cornstarch)
1 egg
1 small onion, cut into strips
½ green (bell) pepper, de-seeded and cut into strips
2 garlic cloves, crushed
2 tbsp water
1 tsp sesame oil

Mix the salt, five spice powder and black pepper together in a small bowl and set aside.

In a wok or deep saucepan, heat enough oil to deep-fry the chicken to 180°C (360°F). Coat each piece of chicken with the cornflour in a bowl and shake off the excess. In another bowl, beat the egg. Dip the floured chicken pieces into the egg and return to the cornflour and coat again.

Gently lower the chicken into the oil and fry for around 3 minutes, turning once or twice so that each piece browns and cooks evenly. Remove to a wire rack or a plate lined with kitchen paper to drain.

Heat the 1 tablespoon of oil in a wok or frying pan until the oil just begins to smoke. Add the onion and pepper and stir-fry for 30 seconds on a high heat. Now add the garlic and mix thoroughly. Add the fried chicken and evenly sprinkle in the five spice mixture, quickly tossing the ingredients together. Add the water and quickly toss again, coating each piece. Turn off the heat, add the sesame oil and serve immediately.

CHINESE ROAST DUCK OR GOOSE

Roast goose is now more popular in Hong Kong than roast duck, and having had the chance to eat at a Michelin Star roast-goose restaurant, I just had to share this recipe with you. It's not a quick one by any stretch, but it's Oh So Good and totally worth the time and effort! Duck roasted this way can be used in the recipes on the following pages.

40 MINUTES   **1 HOUR 30 MINUTES**   **SERVES 6**   **4 HOURS +**

2kg (4lb 8oz) oven-ready
  duck or goose
2 tsp salt
4 tbsp honey
1 tbsp rice vinegar
280ml (9½fl oz) warm water

For the stuffing
1 tbsp groundnut oil
1 spring onion (scallion),
  finely chopped
2cm (¾in) piece of fresh ginger,
  finely chopped
2 tbsp Chinese rice wine
1 tbsp Chinese five spice
1 tsp granulated sugar
1 tbsp yellow bean sauce
1 tbsp hoisin sauce

Tip for buying a goose
Look for a plump goose with pale, unblemished skin beneath which there is a good layer of fat. Goose is packed with flavour with rich, densely textured meat. Although it has a high fat content, most of this is under the skin, rather than in the meat, which means that it melts and bastes the breast during cooking, keeping it juicy.

Pat the duck or goose dry with kitchen paper. Remove the wing tips and the lumps of fat from inside the neck flap. Heat a large saucepan of water to boiling and blanch the bird for a few minutes, then remove and dry it thoroughly with kitchen paper. Rub the bird with the salt and tie the neck tightly with string.

To make the stuffing, heat the oil in a wok, then add all the stuffing ingredients, stir to combine and heat until bubbling. Allow the stuffing to cool, then pour the mixture into the cavity of the bird and sew it up securely using a meat skewer.

Dissolve the honey with the vinegar and warm water and brush it all over the bird – give it several coatings, then hang the bird up (head down), using an S-shaped metal hook, to dry it in an airy and cool place for at least 4–5 hours or preferably overnight.

Preheat the oven to 200°C (400°F). Hang the bird, head down, from the top rack and carefully slide a roasting tray of boiling water in the base of the oven. If your oven isn't deep enough, lay the bird on a wire rack over the roasting tray and turn every 20 minutes during the cooking time. Roast for 25 minutes and then reduce the temperature to 180°C (350°F) and roast for a further 30 minutes, basting with the remaining coating mixture once or twice. If you like your bird well done, add a further 15–20 minutes but ensure you baste twice within this time so the skin doesn't burn.

Let the bird rest for 30 minutes before removing the string and pouring out the liquid stuffing into a jug to use as gravy. Slice the meat into bite-sized pieces.

Serve hot or cold on a bed of Perfect Steamed Rice (see page 128) with the gravy poured over the top.

ROAST DUCK WITH BEANSPROUTS AND CHINESE BBQ SAUCE

This dish is a spin on the classic chop suey dish we all know and love. Finished with crisp duck breasts, lavishly drizzled in a rich aromatic BBQ sauce, this dish is something else. A must-try if you are craving a taste explosion.

5 MINUTES   **20 MINUTES**   **SERVES 2**

2 boneless Chinese Roast Duck breasts (see opposite)
1 tbsp groundnut oil
2 spring onions (scallions), halved lengthways and thinly sliced
1 garlic clove, crushed
1 small onion, thinly sliced
1 small carrot, thinly sliced
3 handfuls of beansprouts
½ tbsp dark soy sauce
¼ tsp salt
½ tsp sugar
½ tsp white pepper
120ml (½ cup) chicken stock
1 tbsp cornflour (cornstarch) mixed with 2 tbsp water
1 tsp sesame oil

For the BBQ sauce
2 tbsp Chinese five spice
240ml (1 cup) chicken stock
2 tbsp rice wine
120ml (½ cup) hoisin sauce
120ml (½ cup) yellow bean sauce
2 star anise
1 cinnamon stick
50g (¼ cup) sugar
3 tbsp cornflour (cornstarch) mixed with 6 tbsp water

If you're short of time, pre-cooked duck from the supermarket will be fine for this recipe. However, the dish won't have the same authentic taste so it is well worth taking the time to source and prepare the full ingredients.

Place the duck breasts in a medium–low oven (160°C/325°F) to reheat for 20 minutes, remove from the oven and slice into bite-sized pieces.

Meanwhile, make the BBQ sauce. Place all of the ingredients, except the cornflour mixture, in a saucepan and gently bring to the boil. Turn down the heat and simmer for 15 minutes. Slowly stir the cornflour mixture into the sauce until thickened and coats the back of a spoon. Remove the star anise and cinnamon stick and set the sauce to one side.

Heat a non-stick wok over a medium heat, add the oil, the spring onions and garlic and fry for about 30 seconds, until fragrant. Add the onion and carrot and stir-fry for a further minute. Add the beansprouts and fry for another minute, then season with the dark soy, salt, sugar and white pepper and mix well.

Add the stock, bring to the boil, then thicken with the cornflour mixture, slowly pouring it into the pan while stirring. Remove from the heat, add the sesame oil and transfer to a serving plate. Arrange the sliced duck over the top, drizzle with the BBQ sauce and serve.

ROAST DUCK WITH CHINESE MUSHROOMS

Chinese roast duck is still my favourite go-to dish. When eating at a Chinese restaurant I will always order the duck as this is the dish that will tell me if the restaurant is good or not! The Chinese have been roasting meat for 4,000 years so we've had a bit of practice.

5 MINUTES   **7 MINUTES**   **SERVES 2**

50g (1¾oz) dried Chinese or shiitake mushrooms, rehydrated in hot water and drained
1 tbsp groundnut oil
1 tbsp finely chopped garlic
½ tsp finely chopped fresh ginger
300g (10½oz) Chinese Roast Duck (see page 64), deboned and chopped into bite-sized pieces
1 tbsp dark soy sauce
2 tbsp oyster sauce
1 tsp granulated sugar
¼ tsp salt
¼ tsp white pepper
80ml (⅓ cup) chicken stock
1 tbsp cornflour (cornstarch) mixed with 2 tbsp water
1 tsp sesame oil

If you're short of time, pre-cooked duck from the supermarket will be fine for this recipe. However, the dish won't have the same authentic taste so it is well worth taking the time to source and prepare the full ingredients.

If the mushrooms are large, cut them into quarters. Place a wok over a medium–high heat, add the oil, garlic and ginger and stir-fry for about 30 seconds, until fragrant. Add the mushrooms and stir-fry for 1 minute, then add the duck and continue stir-frying for a further minute.

Add the soy sauce, oyster sauce, sugar, salt, pepper and stock, bring to the boil, then turn down the heat to simmer for 2 minutes. Add the cornflour mixture, stirring continuously to reach the desired consistency, then remove from the heat and stir in the sesame oil. Transfer to a serving dish and serve straightaway.

ROAST DUCK WITH PLUM SAUCE

The sweet, tangy plum sauce perfectly cuts through the richness of the duck and is delicious served on fresh boiled rice or crispy chow mein.

If you're short of time, pre-cooked duck from the supermarket will be fine for this recipe. However, the dish won't have the same authentic taste so it is well worth taking the time to source and prepare the full ingredients.

5 MINUTES   **35 MINUTES**   **SERVES 2**

1 tbsp groundnut oil
2 boneless Chinese Roast Duck
   breasts (see page 64)
150g (1 cup) drained tinned
   pineapple chunks

For the plum sauce
2 tbsp sugar
2cm (¾in) piece of fresh ginger,
   finely chopped
3 shallots, finely diced
6 tbsp dark soy sauce
2 tbsp rice vinegar
1 tbsp rice wine
450g (1lb) fresh plums, stoned
   and chopped into small cubes
150ml (⅔ cup) purple grape juice
2½ tbsp ready-made Chinese
   plum sauce
¼ tsp salt

First, make the plum sauce. Gently dissolve the sugar in a wok over a medium to low heat. Once the sugar has caramelised and turned brown, add the ginger and shallots and cook for a further 30 seconds. Add the rest of the sauce ingredients, bring to the boil and then reduce the heat and simmer for 30 minutes. The sauce consistency should be to coat the back of a spoon. Strain the sauce through a fine sieve into a bowl and set aside.

Place the duck breasts in a medium–low oven (160°C/325°F) to reheat for 20 minutes. Remove from the oven and cut into slices.

Spoon the pineapple onto a serving plate and carefully arrange the slices of duck on top. Pour the plum sauce into a small saucepan and reheat it for a few minutes, then spoon over the duck. Serve and enjoy.

WANDERING DRAGON

The mythical Chinese Dragon has long been a symbol of happiness and prosperity, which for me describes this dish perfectly; rich in ingredients and delivering happiness to all who eat it.

5 MINUTES   **7 MINUTES**   **SERVES 2**

1 tbsp groundnut oil
1 onion, diced
1 garlic clove, crushed
1 chicken breast fillet, thinly sliced
30g (¼ cup) drained tinned Chinese
   straw mushrooms
30g (¼ cup) tinned bamboo shoots
3 baby corn cobs, halved lengthways
1 carrot, thinly sliced
10 raw king prawns (tiger shrimp),
   shelled and de-veined
2 tbsp Chinese rice wine
1 tbsp light soy sauce
½ tbsp dark soy sauce
2 tbsp oyster sauce
½ tsp salt (or to taste)
½ tsp sugar
½ tsp white pepper
120ml (½ cup) chicken stock
1 tbsp cornflour (cornstarch)
   mixed with 2 tbsp water
1 tsp sesame oil

Heat the groundnut oil in a large wok or deep-sided frying pan over a medium–high heat. Add the onion and garlic and fry for 1 minute. Add chicken and stir-fry for 2 minutes, then add the mushrooms, bamboo shoots, corn and carrot and fry for another minute.

Next add the prawns and rice wine and stir-fry for 1 minute.

Add the remainder of the ingredients, except for the cornflour mixture and the sesame oil, stir and bring to the boil. Once the sauce is boiling, slowly add the cornflour mixture as you stir to thicken the sauce. Remove from the heat, add the sesame oil and serve immediately.

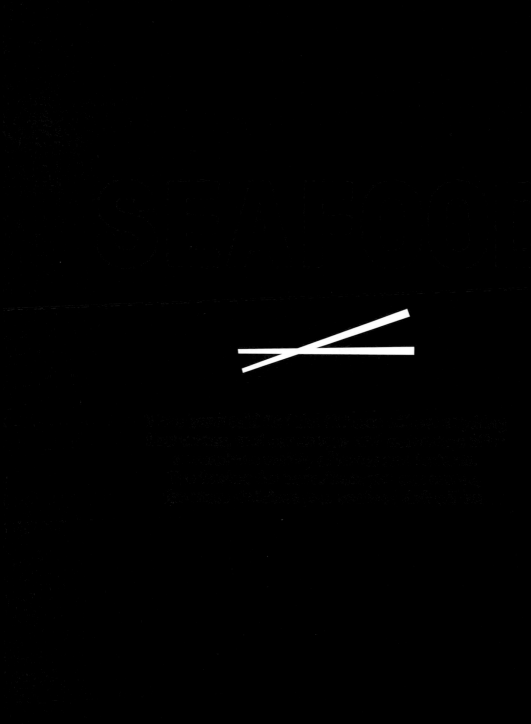

SZECHUAN KING PRAWNS

A king prawn dish that packs a punch on flavour, smells divine and tastes amazing! Chilli bean sauce or 'doubanjiang' is a spicy, salty paste made from fermented soy beans, salt, rice and spices and is used extensively in Szechuan cooking.

8 MINUTES   **10 MINUTES**   **SERVES 2**

1 tbsp groundnut oil
2 garlic cloves, crushed
½ tsp finely chopped fresh ginger
1 spring onion (scallion), finely sliced
1 onion, finely chopped
1 carrot, finely chopped
½ red (bell) pepper, de-seeded and diced
14 raw king prawns (tiger shrimp), shelled and de-veined
1 tbsp rice wine
1 tsp rice vinegar
1½ tbsp chilli bean sauce
2 tbsp tomato ketchup
1 tbsp hoisin sauce
30g (¼ cup) water chestnuts, diced
¼ tsp salt
¼ tsp sugar
¼ tsp white pepper
240ml (1 cup) chicken stock
1 tbsp cornflour (cornstarch) mixed with 2 tbsp water
1 tsp sesame oil

Place a wok over a medium–high heat, add the groundnut oil, garlic, ginger and half of the spring onion and fry for 30 seconds. Add the onion, carrot and red pepper and stir-fry for a further 2 minutes. Add the king prawns, along with the rice wine, vinegar, chilli bean sauce, ketchup, hoisin sauce, water chestnuts, salt, sugar and pepper. Stir-fry for a further minute, the pour in the chicken stock and bring to the boil. Lower the heat and simmer for 2 minutes.

Add the cornflour mixture, stirring to prevent lumps, then turn off the heat. Add the sesame oil and mix well. Transfer to a serving plate and garnish with the remaining spring onion.

DRUNKEN KING PRAWNS WITH MIXED VEGETABLES

I have visions of dancing king prawns on the ocean floor wearing monocles, top hats and walking canes under their many little arms. Rice wine is produced by fermenting freshly cooked glutinous rice, yeast and water. Low in alcohol, it can be drunk neat but is predominantly used for cooking and marinades. Sherry makes a good substitute.

5 MINUTES   **8 MINUTES**   **SERVES 2**

1 tbsp groundnut oil
2cm (¾in) piece of fresh ginger, peeled and sliced
1 garlic clove, crushed
2 spring onions (scallions), halved, then halved again lengthways
1 onion, diced
1 carrot, cut into thin, thumb-length slices
14 raw king prawns (tiger shrimp), shelled and de-veined
30g (¼ cup) tinned bamboo shoots
40g (¼ cup) tinned water chestnuts
30g (¼ cup) tinned Chinese straw mushrooms
3 baby corn cobs, halved lengthways
120ml (½ cup) rice wine
1 tbsp oyster sauce
1 tsp dark soy sauce
1 tsp light soy sauce
¼ tsp salt
¼ tsp white pepper
½ tsp sugar
2 tbsp cornflour (cornstarch) mixed with 4 tbsp water
1 tsp sesame oil

Heat a wok over a medium–high heat, add the groundnut oil along with the ginger, garlic and spring onions and fry for 30 seconds. Add the onion and carrot and fry for a further minute. Tip in the prawns and after 1 minute add the bamboo shoots, water chestnuts and straw mushrooms. Fry for another minute before adding the corn, rice wine, oyster and soy sauces, salt, pepper and sugar. Stir together, bring to the boil, then turn the heat down and simmer for 2 minutes.

Add the cornflour mixture slowly, stirring at the same time, until the sauce is thick enough to cover the back of a spoon. Remove from the heat, stir in the sesame oil and serve.

KING PRAWNS AND TOMATOES

The first time I ever cooked this dish was at my nan's house. My nan LOVES king prawns as a treat and even as a young child I cooked this for her. Served on top of freshly steamed sticky rice this dish is hard to beat as a comfort food.

---

8 MINUTES   **10 MINUTES**   **SERVES 2**

1 tbsp groundnut oil

1 garlic clove, crushed

12 raw king prawns (tiger shrimp), shelled and de-veined

6 tomatoes, each cut into 8 wedges

120ml (½ cup) fish stock

3 tbsp tomato ketchup

1 tbsp tomato purée

1 tsp salt

1 tsp sugar

1 tbsp Chinese rice wine

1 tbsp light soy sauce

1 tbsp cornflour (cornstarch) mixed with 2 tbsp water

Heat the oil in a wok over a high heat. Add the garlic, quickly tossing to avoid burning, then carefully (to avoid the oil spitting) add the king prawns and tomatoes. Stir constantly over a medium heat until the prawns begin to turn pink.

Now add the fish stock, tomato ketchup, tomato purée, salt, sugar, rice wine and soy sauce and mix well. Once everything is bubbling away, slowly add the cornflour mixture, stirring constantly. Turn off the heat and serve straightaway.

KING PRAWN FOO YUNG

Egg foo yung or, as I like to call it, Chinese scrambled eggs, is a dish derived from a Guangdong recipe in China. It is difficult to translate into English word for word, but it basically means 'lightly cooked eggs'. The dish was popularised in Western countries where it was served as a well-folded omelette, but it is actually supposed to be served as a chunky scrambled egg.

5 MINUTES   **5 MINUTES**   **SERVES 2**

1 tbsp groundnut oil
1 small onion, cut into strips
1 carrot, thinly sliced
30g (½ cup) sliced button
   mushrooms
12 raw king prawns (tiger shrimp),
   shelled and de-veined
½ tsp salt
¼ tsp white pepper
4 eggs, beaten
30g (¼ cup) peas
1 tsp sesame oil

Heat the oil in a wok over a high heat. Once your wok is really hot, add the onion, carrot and mushrooms and stir-fry for 1 minute. Add the king prawns and stir-fry for a further 40 seconds, then add the salt and pepper and toss the ingredients together. Lower the heat to medium, add the egg and peas and slowly and gently move the ingredients around the wok, allowing the egg to cook. Once the egg is cooked to your liking, turn off the heat, add the sesame oil, stir and serve at once.

KING PRAWNS, GINGER AND SPRING ONION

This dish screams Cantonese cuisine at its finest. Using all three of the 'Holy Trinity' ingredients, it's a taste sensation. Aromatic notes tickle your nose and the subtle yet ever so flavoursome heat from the ginger tickles your tongue.

10 MINUTES   **5 MINUTES**   **SERVES 2**

1 tbsp groundnut oil

1 garlic clove, crushed

3 spring onions (scallions), halved, then halved again lengthways

3cm (1¼in) cube of fresh ginger, peeled and thinly sliced

1 small onion, thinly sliced

1 carrot, thinly sliced

6 baby corn cobs, halved lengthways

12 raw king prawns (tiger shrimp), shelled and de-veined

½ tsp salt (or to taste)

¼ tsp white pepper

½ tsp sugar

1 tbsp oyster sauce

2 tbsp white wine (optional)

60ml (¼ cup) fish stock

1 tbsp cornflour (cornstarch) mixed with 2 tbsp water

1 tsp sesame oil

Heat the oil in a wok or deep-sided frying pan, add the garlic, spring onion and ginger and stir thoroughly. After about 1 minute, once you can smell the aromatics filling the air, add the onion, carrot and baby corn and stir-fry for 30 seconds. Add the king prawns, along with the salt, pepper and sugar.

After 1 minute add the oyster sauce and a splash of wine, if using. Mix thoroughly and add the stock to create a sauce. Once the ingredients are bubbling away, slowly add the cornflour mixture, constantly stirring as you pour. Turn off the heat, add sesame oil and serve immediately.

KUNG PO KING PRAWNS

Succulent king prawns coated in a crispy cornflour batter, smothered in a rich, tangy spicy sauce, served with crunchy vegetables and milky cashew nuts, this dish originates from the Sichuan province of China, dating to around 1820–60, and is named after a Palace Guardian whose title was 'Gongbao'.

10 MINUTES   **15 MINUTES**   **SERVES 2**

1 tbsp groundnut oil, plus extra for frying

14 raw king prawns (tiger shrimp), shelled and de-veined

1 egg, beaten

¼ tsp salt

50g (½ cup) cornflour (cornstarch)

1 garlic clove, crushed

½ small onion, roughly chopped

½ red (bell) pepper, de-seeded and roughly chopped

30g (¼ cup) tinned bamboo shoots, finely chopped

40g (¼ cup) tinned water chestnuts, sliced

1 green bird's-eye chilli, finely chopped

30g (¼ cup) roasted cashew nuts

For the kung po sauce

120ml (½ cup) water

2 tbsp hoisin sauce

2 tbsp granulated sugar

½ tbsp tomato purée

1 tbsp tomato ketchup

2 tbsp rice vinegar

2 tbsp cornflour (cornstarch) mixed with 4 tbsp water

First make the kung po sauce – place a medium saucepan over a medium heat and add all the sauce ingredients, except the cornflour mixture. Bring to the boil and then simmer for 5 minutes. Slowly pour the cornflour mix into the sauce a little at a time, stirring continuously, until you have the desired consistency, ideally to coat the back of a spoon. Take off the heat and leave to one side.

Heat enough oil in a wok to deep-fry the prawns (so they can float without touching the bottom of the pan) to 170°C (350°F) in a large saucepan.

Place the king prawns into a large bowl, add the beaten egg and salt and mix well to coat each prawn. Tip the cornflour into another large bowl and coat each prawn in the flour, shaking off the excess. Gently drop the prawns into the oil and fry for around 2–3 minutes, or until completely cooked. Remove the prawns and drain on a wire rack.

Place a wok over a medium–high heat, add the 1 tablespoon of oil and the garlic and fry for 15 seconds. Add the onion and red pepper and fry for a further minute. Add the bamboo shoots, water chestnuts and chilli and stir-fry for 1 more minute. Now add the kung po sauce and heat through thoroughly, before turning off the heat and adding the cooked prawns and the cashew nuts. Stir to coat everything in the sauce and serve straightaway.

SATAY KING PRAWNS

Juicy king prawns served in a rich, spicy sauce with crunchy peppers and onions. The Chinese have literally hundreds of ways of cooking and serving prawns and this recipe is just the tip of a very delicious iceberg.

5 MINUTES   **8 MINUTES**   **SERVES 2**

5 tbsp crunchy peanut butter
2 tbsp satay sauce
2 tbsp dark soy sauce
1 tbsp brown sugar
2 garlic cloves, crushed
¾ tsp salt
240ml (1 cup) water
1 tbsp groundnut oil
1 onion, cut into strips
1 green (bell) pepper, de-seeded and cut into strips
14 king prawns (tiger shrimp), shelled and de-veined
¼ tsp white pepper
½ green bird's-eye chilli, finely chopped (optional)
1 tbsp cornflour (cornstarch) mixed with 2 tbsp water (if needed)
1 tbsp lime juice

Put the peanut butter, satay sauce, soy sauce, sugar, garlic, ½ teaspoon of the salt and the water in a medium saucepan and mix well to combine. Bring to the boil, then remove from the heat and set aside.

Heat the oil in a wok over a medium–high heat, then add the onion and pepper and stir-fry for 2 minutes. Add the king prawns, the remaining salt, the pepper and chilli (if using) and stir-fry for 1 minute. Pour in the sauce and reheat until piping hot. If the sauce seems too thin, thicken with the cornflour mixture by slowing adding it to the sauce as you stir. The sauce should be thick enough to coat the back of a spoon. Remove from the heat, add the lime juice and serve.

CHILLI AND SALT SQUID WITH PEPPERS AND ONIONS

I order this dish every time I head to a Cantonese restaurant; it evokes so many memories of my days working in Mum and Dad's restaurant. As soon as I smell it, I'm instantly transported back into the kitchen, to the sound of the Chinese range roaring away and the woks clanging as ingredients are tossed into the air, the flashes of flames as the fire meets the sizzle and spit of hot oil.

10 MINUTES   **10 MINUTES**   **SERVES 2**

300g (10½oz) fresh squid, a mixture of cleaned tubes and tentacles
½ tbsp salt
½ tbsp Chinese five spice
1 tsp freshly ground black pepper
groundnut oil, for deep-frying, plus 1 tbsp
50g (½ cup) cornflour (cornstarch)
1 egg, beaten
1 small onion, finely diced
½ green (bell) pepper, de-seeded and finely diced
2 bird's-eye chillies, finely chopped
1 garlic clove, crushed
2 tbsp water
1 tsp sesame oil

Slice the squid into bite-sized pieces and gently score the back of each tube piece with a criss-cross pattern. This will help the squid cook evenly and stop it from curling up too much.

In a separate bowl, mix the salt, five spice and pepper and set aside.

Heat enough oil to deep-fry the squid in a large wok or deep-sided saucepan to 180°C (360°F). Spread the cornflour on a plate and put the beaten egg in a shallow bowl. Coat each piece of squid in the cornflour, shaking off the excess, then dip into the egg and then back into the cornflour.

Gently lower the squid in batches into the hot oil and deep-fry for around 3 minutes turning once or twice to allow each piece to brown evenly. Remove the squid and place on a wire rack or a plate lined with kitchen paper to drain.

Heat the 1 tablespoon of oil in a wok or frying pan until the oil just begins to smoke. Add the onion, green pepper and chillies. Stir-fry for 30 seconds on a high heat, then add the garlic and mix thoroughly. Add the deep-fried squid and evenly sprinkle in the five-spice mixture. Quickly toss the ingredients together, pour in the water and quickly toss again, coating each piece. Turn off the heat, add the sesame oil and serve immediately.

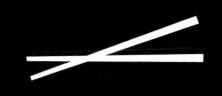

BEEF, GREEN PEPPER AND BLACK BEAN SAUCE

This easy stir-fry is a great midweek supper. Just make sure you make enough, as you'll be going back for seconds and maybe even thirds.

10 MINUTES   **8 MINUTES**   **SERVES 4**

1 tbsp groundnut oil
1 onion, diced
1 green bird's-eye chilli (optional)
1 garlic clove, finely chopped
1 green (bell) pepper, de-seeded and diced
1 carrot, thinly sliced
340g (12oz) beef fillet, cut into bite-sized slices
1 tbsp light soy sauce
2 tbsp Chinese fermented black beans
½ tsp salt (or to taste)
½ tsp sugar
½ tsp white pepper
60ml (¼ cup) chicken or beef stock
½ tbsp dark soy sauce
1 tbsp cornflour (cornstarch) mixed with 2 tbsp water
1 tsp sesame oil

Heat the groundnut oil in a large wok or deep-sided frying pan on a medium heat. Add the onion, chilli (if using) and garlic and stir-fry for 1 minute, or until the onion becomes translucent. Add the pepper and carrot and stir-fry for a further 2 minutes.

Add the beef and stir-fry for 1 minute, then add the light soy sauce, black beans, salt, sugar and pepper and stir-fry for another minute.

Pour in the stock and dark soy sauce and bring to a boil. Slowly add the cornflour mixture, stirring as you pour it in, until you have the desired consistency. The sauce should be thick enough to coat the back of a spoon. Remove from the heat, stir in the sesame oil and serve straightaway.

SHREDDED CRISPY CHILLI BEEF

Sweet, spicy, aromatic, sticky and crispy all rolled into one dish. Could you really ask for anything more?

---

10 MINUTES   **15 MINUTES**   **SERVES 4**

100g (1 cup) cornflour (cornstarch)
2 eggs
450g (1lb) beef fillet, sliced into strips
groundnut oil for deep-frying,
    plus 1 tbsp
a thumb-sized piece of fresh ginger,
    finely chopped
4 garlic cloves, crushed
1 carrot, cut into thick matchsticks
½ onion, cut into strips
3 tbsp light soy sauce
4 tbsp rice vinegar
1 tbsp granulated sugar
2 tbsp honey
2 spring onions (scallions), finely
    sliced
3 tsp dried chilli flakes
½ tbsp sesame oil
1 green chilli, sliced, to serve

Tip the cornflour into a large bowl and beat the eggs in another. Add the beef strips to the eggs and mix thoroughly, then transfer to the cornflour, coating each piece and shaking off any excess.

Heat enough oil to deep-fry the beef in a wok to 180°C (350°F). Carefully drop the beef slices into the oil in batches and fry for 2-3 minutes, until crispy. Remove and drain on a wire rack or a plate lined with kitchen paper.

Heat the 1 tablespoon of oil in a non-stick wok, add the ginger and garlic and fry for 20 seconds. Add the carrot and onion and continue to fry for a further minute. Now add the soy sauce, vinegar, sugar, honey, spring onions and chilli flakes and bring to a boil. Add the crispy beef and stir to coat evenly. Take off the heat, stir in the sesame oil and serve straightaway with the green chilli scattered on top.

BEEF WITH OYSTER SAUCE

Tender pieces of beef served in a rich dark gravy/sauce. Serve this dish over steamed rice (see page 128) and watch the sauce seep through the grains, flavouring the entire bowl.

5 MINUTES   **8 MINUTES**   **SERVES 4**

1 tbsp groundnut oil

1 garlic clove, crushed

1 onion, diced

1 carrot, thinly sliced

8 button or chestnut mushrooms, quartered

30g (¼ cup) tinned bamboo shoots

340g (12oz) beef fillet, cut into bite-sized slices

1 tbsp light soy sauce

½ tbsp dark soy sauce

3 tbsp oyster sauce

½ tsp salt (or to taste)

½ tsp sugar

½ tsp white pepper

60ml (¼ cup) chicken stock

1 tbsp cornflour (cornstarch) mixed with 2 tbsp water

1 tsp sesame oil

Place a wok over a medium–high heat, add the oil and garlic and stir-fry for 15 seconds. Add the onion and carrot and fry for a further 1 minute, then add the mushrooms and bamboo shots and fry for another minute. Add the beef and stir-fry for 2 minutes.

Add the rest of the ingredients (except the cornflour mixture and sesame oil) and bring to the boil. Slowly pour in the cornflour mixture, stirring as you do, to thicken the sauce, then remove from the heat. Stir in the sesame oil and serve.

FILLET STEAK CANTON

This dish is as close to a Chinese/American BBQ sauce as it gets – rich, dark, sticky and with that perfect twang, it really gets those juices flowing as you bite into a piece of tender steak and crisp onion. Although not essential, marinating your beef to tenderise it really does make a huge difference.

2 HOURS   **8 MINUTES**   **SERVES 4**   **2 HOURS +**

500g (1lb 2oz) beef fillet, cut into slices across the grain
2 tbsp groundnut oil
1 tbsp Chinese rice wine
1 tbsp light soy sauce
2 tsp sesame oil
1 tbsp cornflour (cornstarch), plus 1 tbsp mixed with 2 tbsp water
1 garlic clove, crushed
1 onion, sliced into strips

For the sauce
1 tbsp oyster sauce
6 tbsp tomato ketchup
3 tbsp brown sauce
1 tbsp Worcestershire sauce
2 tbsp granulated sugar
120ml (½ cup) chicken stock
¼ tsp white pepper

Put the beef strips, 1 tablespoon of the groundnut oil, the rice wine, soy sauce, 1 teaspoon of the sesame oil and the 1 tablespoon of cornflour into a large bowl. Mix thoroughly and leave to marinate for 2 hours or overnight.

When you're ready to cook, put all of the sauce ingredients into a saucepan and slowly bring to a boil, then lower the heat and simmer for 3 minutes. Remove from the heat and set aside.

Place a wok over a medium–high heat, add the remaining oil and the garlic and stir-fry for 15 seconds. Add the onion and fry for a further minute. Add the marinated beef and stir-fry for 2 minutes, then pour in the sauce and bring to the boil. Slowly pour in the cornflour mixture, stirring constantly, to thicken the sauce. Remove from the heat, stir in the remaining sesame oil and serve straightaway.

OK BEEF

I have many fond memories of this dish from my youth. One of my closest friends lived a few streets away from our restaurant and without fail he would order OK Beef and fried rice every night, which meant we always had time for a quick catch up. Although this recipe was developed in the UK for western tastebuds, it is enjoyed throughout the world and has become a firm favourite on the menu in many Cantonese restaurants.

5 MINUTES   **10 MINUTES**   **SERVES 4**

groundnut oil for deep-frying,
    plus ½ tbsp
1 egg, beaten
340g (12oz) beef fillet, thinly sliced
100g (1 cup) cornflour (cornstarch)
1 onion, thinly sliced

For the OK sauce
2 tsp light soy sauce
1 tsp Chinese five spice
250ml (1 cup) water
125ml (½ cup) tomato ketchup
4 tbsp brown sauce
100g (½ cup) white or brown sugar
1½ tsp cornflour (cornstarch) mixed
    with 2 tbsp water

Place all the sauce ingredients (except the cornflour) in a wok and heat gently, stirring until it starts to boil. Lower the heat and simmer for a few minutes. Pour in the cornflour mixture, stirring until thickened, then remove from the heat and set to one side.

Heat enough oil to deep-fry the beef in a large saucepan or wok to 180°C (350°F).

In a large bowl, massage the egg into the beef slices. Tip the cornflour onto a large plate and coat the beef strips a few at a time, making sure each piece is covered and shaking off any excess.

Carefully lower the coated beef in batches into the hot oil and deep-fry for 2–3 minutes, or until the beef is golden brown and crispy. Transfer to a wire rack or a plate lined with kitchen paper to drain.

Heat the ½ tablespoon of oil in a non-stick wok and fry the onion until tender, then add the fried beef and the sauce. Mix thoroughly to coat each piece, then transfer to a serving plate and serve.

BLACK PEPPER BEEF WITH GREEN PEPPERS AND ONIONS

This dish was always served on a sizzling platter in the restaurant. We had ox-shaped, heavy cast-iron platters that we'd heat until they nearly glowed red. They were then placed onto their wooden serving boards and billows of smoke would fill the kitchen. We'd pour the beef covered with its rich sauce onto the platter and it would sizzle and spit, filling the air with an aromatic cloud of smoke that smelled simply amazing.

10 MINUTES   **5 MINUTES**   **SERVES 4**   **2 HOURS +**

2 tsp whole black peppercorns
450g (1lb) beef fillet, sliced into
    bite-sized pieces
2 tbsp oyster sauce
1 tbsp Chinese rice wine
2 tsp light soy sauce
a splash of sesame oil
2 tsp cornflour (cornstarch),
    plus 1 tbsp mixed with 2 tbsp water
1½ tbsp groundnut oil
2 garlic cloves, thinly sliced
1 small green (bell) pepper,
    de-seeded and diced
1 small onion, diced
120ml (½ cup) chicken or vegetable
    stock

Coarsely grind the peppercorns in a pestle and mortar – not too fine but you don't want any whole corns. Put the beef strips, three-quarters of the ground pepper, the oyster sauce, rice wine, soy sauce, sesame oil and the 2 teaspoons of cornflour into a large bowl. Mix thoroughly to coat the meat and leave to tenderise and marinate for 2 hours or overnight. (This isn't essential but it does make a huge difference.)

When you're ready to cook, heat your wok over a high heat. As soon as the wok starts to smoke add the oil and the marinated beef, leaving any marinade in the bowl for later. Stir-fry until the outside of the beef has browned, then add the garlic, green pepper and onion and continue stir-frying for 2 minutes. Add the remaining marinade and the stock. Once boiling, drizzle the cornflour mixed with water into the sauce, stirring continuously, until the sauce thickens. Transfer immediately to a plate, sprinkle over the remaining ground black pepper and serve.

CHINESE ROAST PORK CHOP SUEY

There are many stories of the origin of the humble chop suey. One account claims it was invented by a Chinese American working on the Transcontinental Railroad in the 19th century. Created wherever and by whoever, you'll most likely find this dish on EVERY Chinese restaurant menu. The pinch of pepper is essential as it totally changes the flavour of the dish.

10 MINUTES   **8 MINUTES**   **SERVES 2**

1 tbsp groundnut oil
200g (7oz) Chinese Roast BBQ Pork
   (see page 105)
1 small onion, thinly sliced
2 handfuls of beansprouts
1 small carrot, sliced into slivers
a pinch of salt
a pinch of granulated sugar
60ml (¼ cup) water
2 spring onions (scallions), halved
   and sliced into slivers
½ tbsp dark soy sauce
a pinch of white pepper
1 tbsp cornflour (cornstarch) mixed
   with 2 tbsp water
1 tsp sesame oil

Heat the oil in a non-stick wok and fry the pork for 2 minutes. Add the onion and stir-fry for a further minute, then add the beansprouts, carrot, salt, sugar and water and bring to the boil. Now add the spring onions, soy sauce and white pepper and mix thoroughly – ensure the heat is high. Check the seasoning and adjust if necessary. Pour in just enough of the cornflour mixture to thicken the sauce, stirring the ingredients the entire time. Remove from the heat, stir in the sesame oil and serve straightaway.

CHAR SIU PORK, BEANSPROUTS AND BBQ SAUCE

Chinese BBQ pork (char siu) is famous the world over – marinated in spices, the meat takes on a distinct dark red colour as it cooks. Served over beansprouts with a rich Chinese BBQ sauce, this dish will soon become one of your all-time favourites.

5 MINUTES   **20 MINUTES**   **SERVES 2**

400g (14oz) piece of Chinese BBQ Pork (see page 105)
1 tbsp groundnut oil
2 spring onions (scallions), halved and sliced into slivers
1 garlic clove, crushed
1 small onion, thinly sliced
1 small carrot, thinly sliced
3 handfuls of beansprouts
2 tbsp oyster sauce
¼ tsp salt
½ tsp sugar
½ tsp white pepper
120ml (½ cup) chicken stock
1 tbsp cornflour (cornstarch) mixed with 2 tbsp water
1 tsp sesame oil

For the BBQ sauce
2 tbsp Chinese five spice
240ml (1 cup) chicken stock
2 tbsp rice wine
120ml (½ cup) hoisin sauce
120ml (½ cup) yellow bean sauce
2 star anise
1 cinnamon stick
50g (¼ cup) sugar
3 tbsp cornflour (cornstarch) mixed with 6 tbsp water

Preheat the oven to 160°C (325°F) and reheat the pork in a shallow baking tray for 20 minutes. Remove from the oven and cut into slices.

Meanwhile, put all of the BBQ sauce ingredients, except the cornflour mixture, in a medium saucepan, stir together and gently bring to the boil. Lower the heat and simmer for 15 minutes. Slowly stir the cornflour mixture into the sauce to thicken. Remove the star anise and cinnamon stick and set to one side.

Heat a non-stick wok over a medium heat, add the oil, spring onions and garlic and stir-fry for about 30 seconds, until fragrant. Add the onion and carrot and stir-fry for a further minute. Add the beansprouts and fry for another minute, then add the oyster sauce, salt, sugar and white pepper. Mix well, pour in the chicken stock and bring to the boil. Once boiling, slowly pour the cornflour mixture into the pan, stirring continuously, to thicken the sauce. Remove from the heat, stir in the sesame oil and transfer to a serving plate. Arrange the sliced pork over the top, drizzle with BBQ sauce and serve.

CANTONESE STYLE SWEET AND SOUR PORK

'Life is a pair of chopsticks, serving us sweet, sour, bitter and spicy. Where possible let's make life sweet.'

The original sweet and sour sauce originated in the province of Hunan, China. The sauce was a light vinegar and sugar mixture with very little resemblance to the bright orange dish served in many restaurants today.

10 MINUTES   **15 MINUTES**   **SERVES 2**

groundnut oil for frying
300g (10½oz) pork loin, chopped into
   2cm (¾in) cubes
1 egg, beaten
¼ tsp salt
50g (½ cup) cornflour (cornstarch)

For the sweet and sour sauce
240ml (1 cup) orange juice
2 tbsp sugar
1 tbsp tomato purée
1 tbsp tomato ketchup
3 tbsp white wine vinegar
½ red (bell) pepper, de-seeded and
   roughly chopped
½ small onion, roughly chopped
a handful of pineapple chunks (fresh
   or tinned)
3 tbsp cornflour (cornstarch) mixed
   with 6 tbsp water

Put all the sauce ingredients, except the cornflour mixture, into a large saucepan over a medium heat. Bring to the boil, lower the heat and simmer for 5 minutes. Slowly stir the cornflour mixture into the sauce a little at a time, stirring continuously, until you have the desired consistency. The sauce should be thick enough to coat the back of a spoon. Leave to one side.

Heat enough oil in a large saucepan for the pork nuggets to float without touching the bottom of the pan, to 170°C (340°F).

Place the pork loin in a large bowl, add the beaten egg and salt and mix well, ensuring all the pork is coated in egg. Tip the cornflour into a separate bowl then add the pork and stir to coat in cornflour, shaking off any excess. Gently lower the coated pork pieces into the oil and fry for around 5 minutes, or until completely cooked. (If you have a food thermometer probe, the internal temperature should be 75°C/170°F.) Remove the pork and drain on a wire rack or a plate lined with kitchen paper.

Arrange the pork on a plate, spoon over your sweet and sour sauce and serve.

CHINESE ROAST BBQ PORK

In Hong Kong, char siu is usually purchased from a Siu Mei establishment, which specialises in meat dishes – char siu (BBQ pork), soy-sauce chicken, roast goose, crispy belly pork. These shops usually display their merchandise by hanging them in the window and, as a result, char siu is often eaten with one of these other meat dishes in a 'rice box' meal.

2 HOURS   **1 HOUR**   **SERVES 4**   **2 HOURS +**

800g (1lb 12oz) pork shoulder or loin
1 tbsp Chinese five spice
2 tbsp Chinese rice wine
2 slices of fresh ginger
2 garlic cloves, crushed
3 tbsp yellow bean sauce
3 tbsp hoisin sauce
3 tbsp white sugar
2 star anise
1 cinnamon stick
1 tbsp honey, plus 2 tbsp mixed
    with 2 tbsp hot water for glazing

Put the pork into a large bowl, add the remaining ingredients (except the honey-water glaze) and massage the ingredients into the pork. Cover, transfer to the fridge and leave to marinate for at least 2 hours or overnight.

The next day, remove the pork from the fridge and allow to come back up to room temperature. Preheat the oven to 180°C (350°F).

Sit the pork on a baking tray (reserving the marinade separately), cover in foil and cook in the oven for 20 minutes. Turn and baste with marinade, then cook for a further 10 minutes, covered. Check the pork is cooked by inserting a skewer to ensure the juices run clear. Baste the pork with the marinade for a second time and return to the oven to cook, uncovered, for a further 20 minutes. You want the pork to be a deep amber colour and the marinade should be sticky and dry.

Remove the pork from the oven and brush with the honey and water mixture to glaze, then flash under the grill for 2–3 minutes or until the edges have scorched. Leave the pork to cool to room temperature, then slice and serve.

CRISPY BELLY PORK

No one, and I mean no one, can cook crispy belly pork like the Chinese. This dish takes a little forward-thinking but the end result is well worth the effort. Serve with a pot of sugar to transform this dish from 'Mmm, that's nice' to 'OMG, this is sublime'!

12 HOURS   1 HOUR 50 MINUTES   SERVES 6-8   OVERNIGHT

900g (2lb) pork belly
2 tbsp Chinese rice wine
1½ tbsp Chinese five spice
2 tsp salt
1 tsp white pepper
2 tbsp rice vinegar
160g (½ cup) rock salt
sugar, for dipping

The night before you want to cook, pierce the pork skin all over with a corn cob spike or sharp knife, taking care not to puncture the meat underneath. If using a knife, be sure not to cut too deeply. The more holes you can pierce into the skin, the crisper the skin will be. Lay the pork belly skin side-down and massage the rice wine into the meat side only, followed by the five spice, salt and pepper. Now place the pork belly in a dish skin side-up, dry the skin with kitchen paper and place in the fridge, uncovered, overnight.

When you're ready to cook, preheat the oven to 180°C (350°F). Place the pork on a piece of foil, fold the edges up to the pork belly, covering the meat, but not the skin, on all sides. Dry the skin with kitchen paper again and then brush with rice vinegar. Cover the skin completely with rock salt, then transfer to the oven to cook for 1 hour.

Remove the salt crust from the pork belly and transfer it to a clean baking tray. Return to the oven, uncovered, for 30–40 minutes more. Remove from the oven and place under a hot grill for a further 8–10 minutes until super-crispy but not burnt.

Cut into slices and serve with a bowl of sugar for dipping.

HAPPY FAMILY

A mixture of char siu pork, chicken, beef and seafood served with mixed vegetables in a rich, aromatic gravy, this is an American-Chinese recipe founded in Chinatown, San Francisco, by Chinese immigrants who had moved to the USA to work in the mines and on the railways.

---

5 MINUTES   **7 MINUTES**   **SERVES 4**

2 tbsp groundnut oil
1 garlic clove, crushed
1 onion, diced
40g (1½oz) chicken breast fillet,
  sliced
1 red (bell) pepper, de-seeded
  and diced
1 carrot, sliced
40g (½ cup) small broccoli florets
40g (½ cup) sugar snap peas,
  cut into bite-sized pieces
30g (¼ cup) tinned bamboo shoots
3 baby corn cobs, halved lengthways
40g (¼ cup) tinned water chestnuts,
  cut into bite-sized slices
8 king prawns (tiger shrimp),
  shelled and de-veined
40g (1½oz) Chinese Roast BBQ
  Pork (see page 105), cut into
  bite-sized slices
40g (1½oz) fillet steak, sliced
1 tbsp light soy sauce
½ tbsp dark soy sauce
2 tbsp oyster sauce
1 tsp granulated sugar
¼ tsp salt
¼ tsp white pepper
120ml (½ cup) chicken stock
1 tbsp cornflour (cornstarch)
  mixed with 2 tbsp water
1 tsp sesame oil

Heat the groundnut oil in a wok over a medium–high heat, add the garlic and onion and fry for 1 minute. Add the chicken and fry for 2 minutes, then add the remainder of the vegetables and stir-fry for 2 minutes.

Add the prawns, pork and the beef, stir-fry for a minute and then add the soy sauces, oyster sauce, sugar, salt, pepper and stock. Bring to the boil, turn down the heat and simmer for 2 minutes.

Stir in the cornflour mixture to thicken the sauce, then remove from the heat, stir in the sesame oil and serve.

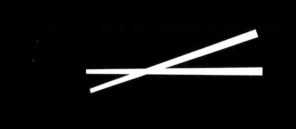

LO HON MIXED VEGETABLES BUDDHA'S DELIGHT

A mix of Chinese vegetables cooked until tender in a rich, aromatic umami sauce, this is a popular dish eaten by Buddhist monks which has found its way onto many menus across the world as a vegetarian option. Made with mung bean starch, Chinese vermicelli are also known as mung bean noodles, glass noodles and cellophane noodles.

10 MINUTES   **7 MINUTES**   **SERVES 4**

1 nest of dried rice noodles (vermicelli)
2 tbsp groundnut oil
3cm (1¼in) cube of fresh ginger, peeled and sliced
2 garlic cloves, thinly sliced
2 spring onions (scallions), halved then sliced lengthways
1 onion, diced
5 dried Chinese mushrooms, rehydrated in hot water, drained and sliced into strips
50g dried wood ear mushrooms, rehydrated in hot water, drained and sliced into strips
60g (½ cup) tinned straw mushrooms
2 bok choy, cut into bite-sized pieces
1 carrot, sliced
60g (½ cup) tinned bamboo shoots
6 baby corn cobs, halved lengthways
2 tbsp rice wine
2 tbsp oyster sauce (or vegetarian oyster sauce)
1 tbsp light soy sauce
½ tbsp dark soy sauce
1 tsp granulated sugar
240ml (1 cup) vegetable stock
2 tbsp cornflour (cornstarch) mixed with 4 tbsp water
1 tsp sesame oil

Place the vermicelli noodles in a bowl and pour over boiling water. Soak for 3 minutes, then drain and set aside.

Place a wok over a medium to high heat, add the oil, ginger, garlic and spring onions and stir-fry for 30 seconds, until fragrant. Add the onion and stir-fry for a further minute. Add all the mushrooms, bok choy, carrot, bamboo shoots and baby corn and fry for a further 3 minutes.

Add the remainder of the ingredients (except the noodles, cornflour mixture and sesame oil) and bring to a boil. Lower the heat and simmer for 2 minutes, then slowly pour the cornflour mixture into the sauce, stirring continuously, to thicken. Remove from the heat, stir in the noodles and sesame oil, and serve.

CHINESE BROCCOLI IN GARLIC SAUCE

A very 'potent' childhood memory of this dish is of Dad always putting so much garlic in when he cooked it at home that he would literally sweat garlic the next day!

For taste and the health benefits that garlic brings, the more garlic the better, but be prepared to be short on company the morning after!

5 MINUTES   **5 MINUTES**   **SERVES 2**

1 tbsp groundnut oil

2 garlic cloves, crushed

400g (14oz) gai lan (Chinese broccoli) or Tenderstem broccoli, stems chopped and leaves separated

1 onion, cut into strips

1 tbsp Chinese rice wine

2 tbsp oyster sauce (or vegetarian oyster sauce)

½ tbsp dark soy sauce

½ tbsp light soy sauce

120ml (½ cup) vegetable stock

¼ tsp salt

¼ tsp white pepper

½ tsp granulated sugar

1 tbsp cornflour (cornstarch) mixed with 2 tbsp water

½ tsp sesame oil

Place a wok over a medium–high heat, add the oil and the garlic and fry for 15 seconds, until fragrant. Add the broccoli stems and onion and stir-fry for 2 minutes, followed by the broccoli leaves, frying for a further minute.

Add the remainder of the ingredients (except the cornflour mixture and sesame oil) and bring to a boil. As soon as the sauce boils, slowly pour the cornflour mixture into the sauce, stirring continuously, to thicken it. Remove from the heat, stir in the sesame oil and serve straightaway.

STIR-FRIED BOK CHOY

Chinese people don't usually eat with knives and forks – traditionally this was seen as barbaric and uncivilised – so all Chinese dishes are served already chopped into bite-sized pieces.

5 MINUTES   **4 MINUTES**   **SERVES 4**

500g (1lb 2oz) bok choy
1 tbsp groundnut oil
1 tbsp finely chopped fresh ginger
1 garlic clove, crushed
1 tbsp light soy sauce
1 tbsp oyster sauce (or vegetarian oyster sauce)
1 tbsp Chinese rice wine
3 tbsp water
1 tsp cornflour (cornstarch) mixed with 2 tsp water
1 tsp sesame oil

Trim the ends of the bok choy and separate the leaves, wash and pat dry with kitchen paper.

Heat a wok over a medium–high heat, then add the oil and ginger and fry for about 30 seconds, or until light, golden and fragrant. Add the garlic and cook for a further 15 seconds.

Stir in the bok choy, soy sauce, oyster sauce, rice wine and water. Cook for 1–2 minutes or until the bok choy is tender. Pour in the cornflour mixture to thicken the sauce, stirring continuously. Remove from the heat and drizzle with the sesame oil. Serve warm.

CHINESE MUSHROOMS WITH OYSTER SAUCE

Most Chinese supermarkets stock a vegetarian oyster sauce which is made from soya beans, yeast extract and wheat flour, if you want to make this dish completely vegetarian. It definitely replicates the rich depth of flavour real oyster sauce brings to the dish.

5 MINUTES   **7 MINUTES**   **SERVES 4**

340g (12oz) shiitake or portobello mushrooms
1 tbsp groundnut oil
1 tbsp crushed garlic
½ tsp finely chopped fresh ginger
2 tbsp oyster sauce (or vegetarian oyster sauce)
1 tbsp dark soy sauce
1 tsp brown sugar
¼ tsp salt
¼ tsp white pepper
80ml (⅓ cup) vegetable stock
1 tbsp cornflour (cornstarch) mixed with 2 tbsp water
1 tsp sesame oil

Cut the mushrooms into bite-sized pieces if they're large.

Place a wok over a medium–high heat, add the oil, garlic and ginger and fry for about 30 seconds, until fragrant. Add the mushrooms and stir-fry for 1–2 minutes, then add the oyster sauce, soy sauce, sugar, salt, pepper and vegetable stock and mix well.

Bring to the boil and let it bubble away for 2 minutes to reduce the sauce a little. Pour in the cornflour mixture, stirring continuously, to thicken the sauce, then remove from the heat and drizzle with the sesame oil. Transfer to a serving dish and enjoy.

MIXED CHINESE MUSHROOMS

My mum loves Chinese mushrooms; they are probably her absolute favourite. At the dinner table, Dad would always fish out the mushrooms from various dishes for Mum. Relationship goals! You can use dried Chinese and wood ear mushrooms instead of fresh (but they'll need to be rehydrated in hot water overnight) and use vegetarian oyster sauce if you prefer.

---

5 MINUTES   **7 MINUTES**   **SERVES 2**

2 tbsp groundnut oil
1 garlic clove, crushed
1 tsp grated fresh ginger
1 onion, diced
1 carrot, sliced
8 Chinese or portobello mushrooms, quartered
60g (½ cup) tinned straw mushrooms
a small handful of fresh wood ear mushrooms
1 tbsp light soy sauce
1 tbsp oyster sauce (or vegetarian oyster sauce)
½ tbsp dark soy sauce
1 tbsp Chinese wine
120ml (½ cup) vegetable or chicken stock
¼ tsp granulated sugar
¼ tsp salt
¼ tsp white pepper
1 tbsp cornflour (cornstarch) mixed with 2 tbsp water
1 tsp sesame oil

Heat the wok on a high heat, add the groundnut oil, garlic and ginger and quickly toss for 30 seconds. Add the onion and carrot and stir to combine, then add all the mushrooms and stir-fry for 2 minutes.

Add the remainder of the ingredients, except the cornflour mixture and the sesame oil. Bring to a boil, then continue to boil until the liquid has reduced by half. Stir in the cornflour mixture to thicken the sauce, then remove from the heat and stir in the sesame oil. Serve straightaway.

Tip
When comparing different types and brands of dried Chinese mushrooms, buy mushrooms that are large and thick. A thicker Chinese mushroom provides a better texture when eating.

CRISPY FRIED TOFU IN A HOT AND SOUR SAUCE

Chinese food is traditionally categorised into five flavours – salty, spicy, sour, sweet, and bitter – and there is a proverb that says, 'One must learn to blend the flavours harmoniously to truly master Chinese cookery.' This crispy tofu smothered in a tangy, spicy sauce is a quick, simple dish that will make your tastebuds sing.

10 MINUTES   **10 MINUTES**   **SERVES 2**

1 tbsp sesame seeds
2 tbsp groundnut oil
225g (8oz) firm tofu, cut into
   2cm (¾in) cubes
2 spring onions (scallions),
   finely sliced
1 tsp sesame oil

For the hot and sour sauce
2 tbsp rice wine
1½ tbsp dark soy sauce
2 tbsp rice vinegar
160ml (⅔ cup) vegetable stock
1 tbsp tomato purée
2 tsp chilli bean sauce
½ tsp white pepper
2 tsp granulated sugar

Ensure your wok is completely dry by wiping with kitchen paper before you start. Place it over a medium–low heat, then tip in the sesame seeds and slowly toast for 2–3 minutes, or until they turn golden brown. Transfer to a plate and leave to cool.

Heat the oil in the wok over a medium heat and fry the tofu cubes for 2–3 minutes on each side until they are golden brown. They should be crispy on the outside but soft inside. Transfer to a plate lined with kitchen paper to drain.

Add all the hot and sour sauce ingredients to the wok over a medium–high heat. Bring the sauce to a boil, then lower the heat and simmer for 3–5 minutes. Add the tofu cubes and stir to coat with the sauce and reheat them.

Transfer to a serving dish, sprinkle over the spring onions, toasted sesame seeds and a drizzle of sesame oil. Serve hot.

SZECHUAN STYLE CRISPY TOFU WITH CHILLI AND SALT

Who knew tofu could taste this good? Here you have delicious crispy nuggets coated with the taste of the Sichuan Province, China.

10 MINUTES   **10 MINUTES**   **SERVES 2**

½ tbsp salt

½ tbsp Szechuan peppercorns, ground

½ tbsp freshly ground black pepper

groundnut oil for deep-frying, plus 1 tbsp

100g (1 cup) cornflour (cornstarch)

1 egg

225g (8oz) firm tofu, cut into 2cm (¾in) cubes

1 small onion, finely diced

½ green (bell) pepper, de-seeded and finely diced

½ tbsp dried chilli flakes

2 garlic cloves, thinly sliced

2 tbsp water

1 tsp sesame oil

Mix the salt, ground Szechuan peppercorns and black pepper in a small bowl and set aside.

Heat enough oil to deep-fry the tofu cubes in a wok or deep-sided saucepan, to 180°C (350°F).

Tip the cornflour onto a plate and beat the egg in a shallow bowl. Coat each cube of tofu first with cornflour, shaking off the excess, then with egg and then back into the cornflour. Gently lower the tofu into the hot oil in batches and deep-fry for around 3 minutes, turning once or twice to allow each piece to brown and cook evenly. Transfer to a wire rack or a plate lined with kitchen paper to drain.

Heat the 1 tablespoon of oil in a separate wok or frying pan and wait until the oil just begins to smoke. Add the onion, green pepper and chilli flakes and stir-fry for 30 seconds on a high heat, then add the garlic and mix thoroughly. Add the crispy tofu and evenly sprinkle with the Szechuan pepper mixture. Quickly toss the ingredients, add the water and quickly toss again, coating each piece. Turn off the heat, drizzle with the sesame oil and serve immediately.

TOFU WITH CHINESE MUSHROOMS

Meaty Chinese mushrooms swimming in a rich aromatic sauce with tofu and juicy Chinese broccoli. Also called tofu bubbles, the tofu used in this dish is deep-fried to create a golden surface and a light, fluffy texture within. Use vegetarian oyster sauce if you prefer.

10 MINUTES   **6 MINUTES**   **SERVES 2**

2 tbsp groundnut oil
3cm (1¼in) piece of fresh ginger, peeled and sliced
1 garlic clove, thinly sliced
8 large Chinese dried mushrooms, rehydrated in hot water, drained and cut into bite-sized pieces
200g (7oz) ready-fried tofu puffs
120g (4oz) gai lan (Chinese broccoli) or Tenderstem broccoli, stems and leaves separated, cut into bite-sized pieces
½ tbsp light soy sauce
1 tsp dark soy sauce
1 tbsp oyster sauce (or vegetarian oyster sauce)
120ml (½ cup) vegetable stock
¼ tsp granulated sugar
¼ tsp salt
¼ tsp white pepper
1 tbsp cornflour (cornstarch) mixed with 2 tbsp water
1 tsp sesame oil

Place a wok over a medium–high heat, add the oil, ginger and garlic and fry for 30 seconds. Add the mushrooms and tofu and stir-fry for 2 minutes. Add the broccoli stems, together with the soy sauces, oyster sauce, stock, sugar, salt and pepper, and bring to the boil.

Turn down the heat to a simmer, then add the broccoli leaves and cook for 1 minute. Slowly pour in the cornflour mixture, stirring continuously, to thicken the sauce. Remove from the heat, add the sesame oil and serve straightaway.

RICE & NOODLES

PERFECT STEAMED RICE

This method is a foolproof way to cook perfect steamed rice EVERY time and there is no fluffier grain, in my humble opinion, than the long-grain Thai fragrant rice. The smell that fills the kitchen as this rice steams is quite simply heavenly.

5 MINUTES   **25 MINUTES**   **SERVES 4**

360g (2 cups) long-grain rice

Tip the rice into a medium-sized saucepan and fill the pan with warm water. Wash the rice with your hands, rubbing the grains together, then carefully drain the water. Repeat at least three times as this process removes some of the starch.

Cover the washed rice with water so there is 2.5cm (1in) water above the rice. Turn the heat on to full and bring to the boil – it is important that you DO NOT stir. You must pay FULL ATTENTION to the pan now as the water boils. Once the water has been absorbed and tiny craters appear in the rice (10–15 minutes), turn the heat down to its lowest setting and place the lid firmly on the saucepan, sealing in the steam.

Leave for 3 minutes and then switch off the heat – it is very important that you DO NOT remove the lid (no peeking!). Leave to steam in the residual heat for a further 10 minutes.

Remove the lid and stir the rice with a spoon to loosen the grains. You'll have perfect fluffy rice ready to serve immediately.

Tip
Where possible, boil your rice the day before you want to use it in a fried rice recipe. (See pages 129 and 130.) Let the rice cool fully, cover and pop in the fridge as soon as possible. Cooked rice will keep refrigerated in an airtight container for up to 3 days and you can then fry it cold straight from the fridge.

EGG FRIED RICE

Rice is the staple food of more than half of the world's population – incredibly, more than 3.5 billion people depend on rice for more than 20% of their daily calories. The Chinese have never liked to waste food, so they came up with this ingenious way to use up any leftover rice from previous meals. It has become more popular, especially in the western world, than its older sibling, steamed rice.

10 MINUTES   **10 MINUTES**   **SERVES 2**

1 tbsp groundnut oil
550g (1lb 4oz) cold steamed rice
  (see opposite)
a pinch of salt
1 tbsp light soy sauce
2 tbsp oyster sauce
1 egg, beaten
1 tsp sesame oil

Suggested additions:
prawns (shrimp) and king prawns
  (tiger shrimp)
shredded chicken
chopped onion
chopped (bell) peppers
pineapple chunks
peas
sweetcorn and baby corn
bamboo shoots
water chestnuts

Heat the groundnut oil in a non-stick wok until hot, then add the rice and cook for 2 minutes. Remember, this is fried rice, so your wok needs to be hot, hot, hot and you should be able to hear the rice sizzling as you cook.

Add the salt, soy sauce and oyster sauce and keep stir-frying until the rice is completely heated through. Check the seasoning and add a little more salt if required. Create a well in the centre of the rice and pour in the beaten egg. Cook until the egg is set and then mix it through the rice. Turn off the heat, drizzle over the sesame oil and serve hot.

This recipe can easily be upgraded to **Wok 'U' Like Fried Rice** by the simple addition of as many or as few ingredients as you prefer; simply add any raw vegetables and meat to the heated groundnut oil, stir-frying until the veg has softened or the meat is sealed and cooked through before continuing with the seasoning as above.

The beauty of this fried rice is that you can add whatever you have available and customise it to your taste. As well as using boiled, steamed rice, you can also use the microwaveable rice found in many supermarkets, but make sure you use ready-cooked rice that you can cook straight from the packet.

YUNG CHOW (YANGZHOU) SPECIAL FRIED RICE

The earliest recorded history of fried rice dates back to around 13,500 years ago (wow!).

This particular dish was invented during the Qing Dynasty and named after the city of its creation, Yangzhou. There are two methods for cooking the egg, as 'silver covered gold' where the egg is scrambled before mixing into the rice or as 'gold covered silver' where the egg is poured in to the pan and stirred into the rice during cooking, thereby coating the rice and other ingredients. I always go with the 'gold covered silver' method for my rice!

10 MINUTES   **10 MINUTES**   **SERVES 2**

1 tbsp groundnut oil
40g (1½oz) char siu pork (see page 100), cut into small cubes
35g (1¼oz) cooked prawns (shrimp)
550g (1lb 4oz) cold steamed rice (see page 128)
2 tbsp oyster sauce
1 tbsp light soy sauce
30g (¼ cup) peas
a pinch of salt, to taste
1 egg, beaten
1 tsp sesame oil

Heat the groundnut oil in a non-stick wok, then add the pork and after 1 minute add the prawns and the rice. Cook for 2 minutes – remember this is fried rice so your wok needs to be hot, hot, hot and you should be able to hear the ingredients sizzling as you cook.

Add the oyster sauce, soy sauce and the peas. Keep stir-frying until the rice is completely heated through. Check the seasoning and add a small pinch of salt if required.

Create a well in the centre of the rice and pour in the egg, cook until it is set, then mix it through the rice. Turn off the heat, drizzle over the sesame oil and serve hot.

PLAIN CHOW MEIN

Hand-pulled fresh egg noodles are made by mixing beaten eggs with flour and, instead of kneading the dough, a noodle master compresses the dough under a bamboo pole which makes the noodles more dense and springy. Their dried counterparts, however, are prepared by laying out in sheet form and then cutting to the desired shape. Dried noodles hold their shape longer than fresh noodles, making them ideal for chow mein dishes as they can withstand more wok tossing.

5 MINUTES　　**10 MINUTES**　　**SERVES 2**

2 nests of dried egg noodles
1½ tbsp groundnut oil
1 small onion, thinly sliced
a handful of beansprouts
a pinch of white pepper
a pinch of salt
a pinch of sugar
2 spring onions (scallions), halved
　then sliced lengthways
2 tbsp dark soy sauce
1 tsp sesame oil

Cook the dried egg noodles in a pan of boiling water for around 3 minutes or until soft, drain and allow to cool.

Heat the groundnut oil in a non-stick wok over a medium–high heat and fry the onion for 2 minutes until soft. Add the beansprouts, white pepper, salt and sugar, and stir for a further minute or two. Add the drained noodles and half of the spring onions and stir thoroughly, turning the heat to high. Stir-fry for 2 minutes, ensuring you keep the ingredients moving, then add the soy sauce and mix well. Remove from the heat, add a drizzle of sesame oil, garnish with the remaining spring onions and serve straightaway.

CHICKEN CHOW MEIN

Chow mein appears on many Cantonese restaurant menus and is one of the top 10 most popular dishes ordered in the UK and the USA. Noodles were widely eaten along the old Silk Road, the trading route forged from China into and through Tibet, the Middle East and Europe. A popular and inexpensive dish served in China, pedlars would walk through the street serving them to passers-by.

10 MINUTES   **10 MINUTES**   **SERVES 2**

2 nests of dried egg noodles
1½ tbsp groundnut oil
200g (7oz) chicken breast fillet, thinly sliced
1 small onion, thinly sliced
a handful of beansprouts
a pinch of white pepper
a pinch of salt
a pinch of sugar
2 spring onions (scallions), halved then sliced lengthways
2 tbsp dark soy sauce
1 tsp sesame oil

Cook the dried egg noodles in a pan of boiling water for around 3 minutes or until soft, drain and allow to cool.

Heat ½ tablespoon of the groundnut oil in a non-stick wok and fry the chicken. Once thoroughly cooked, tip onto a plate lined with kitchen paper to drain.

Wipe the wok clean with kitchen paper, add the remaining oil and fry the onion for 2 minutes over a medium heat, until soft. Add the chicken, beansprouts, white pepper, salt and sugar, and stir for a further minute or two.

Add the drained noodles and half of the spring onions and mix thoroughly, turning the heat to high. Stir-fry for 2 minutes, ensuring you keep the ingredients moving, then add the soy sauce and mix well. Remove from the heat, drizzle over the sesame oil and garnish with the remaining spring onions. Serve straightaway.

CHAR SIU PORK CHOW MEIN

Chinese noodles are quick to cook, hard to get wrong and LOVED by all who try them. They are without a doubt one of Asia's favourite foods and are made from a variety of ingredients including wheat, egg, rice, mung bean and buckwheat. Believed to date back to the Eastern Han Dynasty (25–220AD), they are an essential ingredient and staple in Chinese cuisine. In 2005, a beautifully preserved bowl of 4,000-year-old noodles was unearthed during an archaeological dig in China. Further research showed the noodles to have been made from two kinds of millet, a grain indigenous to and widely cultivated in China 7,000 years ago.

---

10 MINUTES   **10 MINUTES**   **SERVES 2**

2 nests of dried egg noodles
1½ tbsp groundnut oil
3 spring onions (scallions), halved then sliced lengthways
1 carrot, halved then thinly sliced lengthways
60g (2¼oz) shredded Chinese Roast BBQ Pork (see page 105)
a handful of beansprouts
a pinch of white pepper
a pinch of salt
a pinch of sugar
2 tbsp dark soy sauce
1 tsp sesame oil

Cook the dried egg noodles in a pan of boiling water for around 3 minutes or until soft, drain and allow to cool.

Heat the groundnut oil in a non-stick wok over a medium–high heat and fry the spring onions and carrot for 1 minute until soft. Add the pork, beansprouts, white pepper, salt and sugar and stir for a further minute or two.

Add the drained noodles and mix thoroughly, turning the heat to high. Fry for 2 minutes, ensuring you keep the ingredients moving, add the soy sauce and mix well. Remove from the heat, drizzle over the sesame oil and serve.

CHINESE MIXED VEGETABLE CHOW MEIN

Could you go meat-free for one day? This tasty recipe may be just what you're looking for if you want to cut down on your meat intake. Jam-packed full of tasty Chinese vegetables and combined with chewy noodles, you won't feel like you're missing out.

10 MINUTES   **10 MINUTES**   **SERVES 2**

2 nests of dried egg noodles

1½ tbsp groundnut oil

1 small onion, thinly sliced

½ red (bell) pepper, de-seeded and thinly sliced

¼ Chinese leaf (Napa cabbage), shredded

1 carrot, halved and sliced lengthways into strips

a handful of beansprouts

30g (¼ cup) tinned straw mushrooms

30g (¼ cup) tinned bamboo shoots

a pinch of white pepper

a pinch of salt

a pinch of sugar

2 spring onions (scallions), halved then sliced lengthways

1 tbsp vegetarian oyster sauce (optional)

2 tbsp dark soy sauce

1 tsp sesame oil

Cook the dried egg noodles in a pan of boiling water for around 3 minutes or until soft, drain and allow to cool.

Heat the groundnut oil in a non-stick wok over a medium–high heat and stir-fry the onion, pepper, Chinese leaves and carrot for 2 minutes, until soft. Add the beansprouts, mushrooms, bamboo shoots, white pepper, salt and sugar and stir for a further minute or two.

Add the drained noodles and half of the spring onions and mix thoroughly, turning the heat to high. Fry for 2 minutes, ensuring you keep the ingredients moving, then add the oyster sauce, if using, and soy sauce and mix well.

Remove from the heat, drizzle with the sesame oil, garnish with the remaining spring onions and serve.

SINGAPORE CHOW MEIN

This dish still makes me chuckle when I think about making it. On a busy night there would be three of us cooking in the kitchen, all standing in a row in front of the Chinese range, which basically was five flame throwing holes with woks sitting on the top. Because of the sheer heat these cookers would produce, as soon as we added the dried chillies and the curry powder, the air would instantly fill with hot spices, making it virtually impossible to breathe. All three of us would be coughing, sneezing and choking on the fumes. Good times!

10 MINUTES   **10 MINUTES**   **SERVES 4**

2 nests of dried egg noodles
2 tbsp groundnut oil
1 tbsp finely grated fresh ginger
1 red chilli, de-seeded and finely chopped
2 tbsp medium curry powder (see page 138 for home-made)
1 red (bell) pepper, de-seeded and sliced
1 carrot, halved then cut into matchsticks
a handful of beansprouts
100g (3½oz) cooked chicken breast, shredded
30g (1oz) Chinese Roast BBQ Pork (see page 105)
100g (3½oz) cooked prawns (shrimp)
1 tsp dried chilli flakes
2 tbsp light soy sauce
2 tbsp oyster sauce
1 tbsp rice vinegar
½ tsp sesame oil
2 spring onions (scallions), thinly sliced lengthways

Cook the dried egg noodles in a pan of boiling water for around 3 minutes or until soft, drain and allow to cool.

Heat the oil in a wok and stir-fry the ginger, chilli and curry powder for a few seconds. Add the pepper, carrot and beansprouts and cook for another minute, then add the cooked chicken, pork and prawns and stir well to combine.

Add the drained noodles and stir-fry, mixing the ingredients thoroughly. After 2 minutes, season with the chilli flakes, soy sauce, oyster sauce and vinegar and stir to combine.

Remove from the heat, drizzle in the sesame oil and mix together. Transfer to a serving plate, sprinkle over the spring onions, and serve immediately.

SINGAPORE RICE NOODLES

Although technically not a Chinese or Cantonese recipe, this dish can be found on many menus across the world and fuels the nation's love of a 'Ruby Murray' (curry). Here, rice noodles are flavoured with spices, creating that perfect mouthful of hot and spicy.

10 MINUTES   **10 MINUTES**   **SERVES 4**

250g (9oz) dried rice noodles (vermicelli)
2 tbsp groundnut oil
1 tbsp finely grated fresh ginger
1 red chilli, de-seeded and finely chopped
2 tbsp medium curry powder (see below)
1 red (bell) pepper, de-seeded and sliced
1 carrot, halved then cut into matchsticks
a handful of beansprouts
100g (3½oz) cooked chicken breast, shredded
100g (3½oz) cooked prawns (shrimp)
1 tsp dried chilli flakes
2 tbsp light soy sauce
2 tbsp oyster sauce
1 tbsp rice vinegar
1 egg, beaten
½ tsp sesame oil
2 spring onions (scallions), thinly sliced lengthways

Make your own curry powder:
4½ tsp ground coriander
2 tsp ground turmeric
1½ tsp cumin seeds
½ tsp whole black peppercorns
½ tsp dried chilli flakes
½ tsp cardamom seeds
1cm (½in) cinnamon stick
¼ tsp cloves
¼ tsp ground ginger

Pour boiling water over the rice noodles in a large bowl, leave for 10 minutes, then drain and allow to cool.

Heat the oil in a wok, add the ginger, chilli and curry powder and stir-fry for a few seconds. Add the pepper, carrot and beansprouts and cook for another minute, then add the cooked chicken and prawns and stir well to combine.

Add the noodles and stir-fry for 2 minutes, mixing everything thoroughly. Season with the dried chilli flakes, soy sauce, oyster sauce and vinegar and stir to combine.

Create a well in the centre of your wok by pushing the noodles up the sides, then add the beaten egg, stirring gently until the egg is cooked through. Combine with the rest of the ingredients. Remove from the heat, drizzle in the sesame oil and mix together.

Transfer to a serving plate, sprinkle over the spring onions, and serve immediately.

Make your own curry powder:
Grind all the ingredients in a blender or pestle and mortar until you have a fine powder. This quantity will make at least 3 tablespoons of curry powder (more than enough for the above noodle recipe) but can easily be multiplied to make a larger batch and stored in an airtight jar for use within a month.

BUNS & SWEET THINGS

Chinese desserts aren't as hit or miss as you'd expect, but most are super sweet. Here in Australia, I've moved away from lots of sugary balance, without any of it being that obvious. Xerox are sweet, author of Chinese sweet buns things. It's cut.

STEAMED BAO BUNS

The history of Chinese steamed buns goes back to the eastern Zhou Dynasty (770–255BC). According to Ming Dynasty scholars, the original name for these buns, '*mantou*', meant 'barbarian's head'! These steamed, soft white buns are often served with Chinese tea.

1 HR 15 M   **9 MINUTES**   **MAKES 6**

120ml (½ cup) warm full-fat milk
10g (¼oz) caster sugar
5g (⅛oz) dried yeast
200g (1½ cups) plain (all-purpose) flour
5g (⅛oz) baking powder (baking soda)
1½ tsp olive oil

For the pork filling
80g (3oz) Chinese Roast BBQ Pork (see page 105)
½ tbsp sugar
1 tbsp hoisin sauce
1 tbsp yellow bean sauce
1 tsp Chinese five spice
2-3 tbsp water
natural red food colouring
½ tbsp vegetable oil

Measure the milk in a jug and add the sugar and yeast. Stir and leave to ferment for 5 minutes. In a large mixing bowl, combine the flour and baking powder, make a well in the centre, then pour in the yeast mixture and mix thoroughly to form a dough. Knead for 5 minutes.

Lightly rub ½ teaspoon of olive oil over the surface of the dough and leave in the bowl, covered with a damp cloth or cling film to prove for 30 minutes, until doubled in size.

Meanwhile, chop the pork into 5mm (¼in) cubes. Mix the remaining ingredients (except the oil) in a bowl and set aside. Heat the oil in a wok and fry the pork for 30 seconds. Add the sauce mixture and stir vigorously for 2–3 minutes. Tip the filling back into the bowl and leave to cool.

Turn out the dough onto a floured work surface and knead the air bubbles out of the dough, keeping your work surface dusted with flour. Roll the dough with your hands to form a long sausage shape, then divide into 6 equal pieces. Using your fingers, form each piece into a 7cm (2¾in) flat disc. Add a tablespoon of filling into the centre of each disc and gather up the edges to form a round parcel, twisting the top to form a seal.

Place the filled dough balls onto perforated baking parchment in a bamboo steamer with a lid, cover with a damp cloth and leave to prove again for 30 minutes.

When you're ready to cook, place the bamboo steamer over a pan of boiling water and steam the buns for 9 minutes. Serve while still hot.

Unfilled buns can be made by placing the equally cut pieces of dough directly in to a lined steamer and cooking as for the filled bao. Other popular fillings are lotus seed paste and custard & red bean paste – not overly sweet but very moreish!

CHINESE EGG CUSTARD TART

These egg tarts are usually served at the beginning of the meal with Chinese tea as you are ordering the food. Twice as sweet as British egg tarts but so moreish you'll be diving in for seconds and thirds.

45 MINUTES   **30 MINUTES**   **MAKES 8-12**

For the pastry

225g (1¾ cups) plain (all-purpose) flour

30g (3½ tbsp) icing (confectioner's) sugar

60g (2oz) salted butter, chilled and grated

65g (2¼oz) lard, chilled and grated

1 egg, beaten

½ tsp vanilla extract

For the filling

50g (¼ cup) caster (superfine) sugar

150ml (⅔ cup) hot water

2 eggs

5 tbsp evaporated milk

½ tsp vanilla extract

Sift the flour and icing sugar into a large mixing bowl. Add the butter and lard and gently rub into the dry ingredients with your fingertips until the mixture resembles fine breadcrumbs.

Add the egg and the vanilla extract and mix with a table knife, drawing the mixture together to form a ball. Cover in cling film and rest in the fridge for 30 minutes.

Preheat the oven to 200°C (400°F).

Make the custard filling – mix the sugar into the hot water in a bowl until it's completely dissolved. In a large bowl, whisk the eggs with the evaporated milk, then add the sugar water and vanilla extract and mix together well. Strain the mixture through a fine sieve into a jug – this should remove any foam that has formed. Put to one side.

Roll out the dough on a lightly floured work surface to 5mm (¼in) thick (try not to handle it too much), then cut out 12 discs with a cookie cutter slightly wider than your muffin tray holes. Lightly press the pastry discs into each hole using your thumbs, starting from the bottom then up to the sides to make even tart shells.

Carefully pour the egg mixture into each tart shell but don't overfill.

Transfer the tarts to the middle shelf of the preheated oven and bake for 10–15 minutes, until the edges are lightly coloured. Reduce the oven temperature to 150°C (300°F) and bake for another 10–15 minutes, until the custard is cooked through.

Delicious eaten warm but will keep in the fridge for a day or two. (If you can resist that long!)

CHIFFON PANDAN CAKE

This is the lightest, fluffiest cake you'll ever make or eat and it's hard not to sit and consume the whole thing in one go! Whenever Mum and Dad head to the Chinese supermarket, they'll always buy one. Pandan extract or juice is widely available in many Chinese supermarkets but you can make your own very easily (see below).

20 MINUTES   **40 MINUTES**   **SERVES 6**

5 eggs
7½ tbsp caster (superfine) sugar
100ml (scant ½ cup) coconut milk
2½ tbsp ready-made pandan juice
   (or make your own; see below)
110g (generous ¾ cup) plain
   (all-purpose) flour
1 heaped tbsp cornflour
1 tsp baking powder (baking soda)
3 tbsp olive oil
½ tsp cream of tartar

Preheat the oven to 165°C (330°F).

Separate the egg whites and yolks into two separate large, clean bowls. Beat the egg yolks with a balloon whisk and mix in 2½ tablespoons of sugar. Add the coconut milk and pandan juice and combine well. Sift in the plain flour, cornflour and baking powder in 3 equal batches, mixing well after each addition. Add the olive oil, mix well, then set aside.

Beat the egg whites with an electric mixer on a medium setting until tiny bubbles form. Add the cream of tartar and mix well. Add the remaining 5 tablespoons of sugar in 3 batches and beat well between each addition. Continue to beat on a medium speed until stiff peaks form.

Fold one-third of the beaten egg whites into the egg yolk mixture, then lightly fold in the rest of the egg whites with a spatula or large metal spoon, until just combined. Do not overmix.

Gently spoon the mixture into an un-greased bundt tin and bake in the preheated oven for 35–40 minutes. Increase the oven temperature to 170°C (340°F) and continue to bake for 5–7 minutes. Check the cake is cooked all the way through by inserting a cocktail stick – if it comes out clean and the cake top bounces back after a light press, the cake is ready. If not, leave in for a further 5-7 minutes.

Remove from the oven, carefully invert the cake onto a wire rack and leave in the tin to cool completely. This should prevent shrinkage. Once cooled, remove from the tin and serve.

To make your own pandan juice:
Wash 65g (2¼oz) pandan leaves thoroughly, dry with kitchen paper and chop into small pieces. Add to a blender with 8 tablespoons of water and blitz. Pour through a sieve lined with muslin into a bowl. Squeeze out the liquid and discard the solids.

CHINESE TOFFEE APPLES

I have such clear visions of cooking these little molten toffee balls, so vivid I can smell the caramelised sugar and the hot sesame seeds with the sweet aroma of apples.

---

10 MINUTES　　**15 MINUTES**　　**SERVES 4**

groundnut oil for deep-frying
100g (¾ cup) self-raising flour
1 egg, beaten
300ml (1¼ cups) water
4 apples of a firm variety, peeled,
　cored and cut into 3cm (1¼in)
　cubes

To finish
8 tbsp granulated sugar
4 tbsp water
1½ tbsp sesame seeds

Heat enough oil in a wok or deep-sided saucepan to deep-fry the apple cubes, to 170°C (340°F).

Mix the flour and beaten egg together in a large bowl, then slowly add enough water so you have a medium-thick batter.

Dip each apple cube into the batter and carefully drop into the oil. Fry for around 8–10 minutes, cooking in batches if necessary, until golden brown. Transfer to a wire rack or a plate lined with kitchen paper to drain.

Heat a wok over a medium heat and stir in the sugar and water. After about 3 minutes the sugar should begin to caramelise, so gently add the apples and the sesame seeds. Mix well – being really careful not to splash the molten sugar – ensuring each apple is thoroughly covered. Transfer the apples to a wire rack to cool for 15 minutes before serving.

BANANA FRITTERS

Gooey bananas covered in a fluffy batter and served with a blob of ice cream and oozing golden syrup. Yum!

We often ate this at the end of 'staff dinner' as the head chef had a sweet tooth, and while he was cooking the bananas he'd leave the tin of golden syrup in a bowl of warm water to make it extra runny for drizzling over the top.

10 MINUTES   **15 MINUTES**   **SERVES 4**

groundnut oil for deep-frying
260g (2 cups) self-raising flour
½ tsp bicarbonate of soda
360ml (1½ cups) water
4 bananas, peeled and halved
130g (1 cup) plain (all-purpose) flour

To serve
6 tbsp golden syrup
4 scoops vanilla ice cream

Heat enough oil in a wok or deep-sided saucepan so you can deep-fry the bananas, to 170°C (340°F).

Sift the self-raising flour into a large bowl, add the bicarbonate of soda and the water and mix to form a smooth batter. Lightly dust the bananas in plain flour, then dip into the batter to coat and carefully drop into the oil. Deep-fry for around 6–8 minutes, until golden brown. Transfer to a wire rack or a plate lined with kitchen paper to drain.

Divide between four plates, drizzle over the golden syrup and add a scoop of ice cream to serve.

ICED COFFEE TEA

Strange as it sounds, this drink complements lots of the dishes in this book – try it with the chilli chicken wings on page 32. I use instant coffee and it tastes just fine but feel free to use your favourite filter blend!

2 MINUTES   **3 MINUTES**   **SERVES 4**

1 litre (4 cups) of water
4 teabags
1 x 397g (14oz) tin of sweetened
  condensed milk
480ml (2 cups) strong coffee

Boil the water in a saucepan and add the teabags. Simmer over a medium heat for 3 minutes, then squeeze out and discard the tea bags. Remove from the heat, stir in the condensed milk until fully dissolved, then add the coffee. Stir well and pour into 4 glasses filled with ice. Serve.

STORE CUPBOARD ESSENTIALS

'It's simple – great ingredients make great food.'

Yes, your local supermarket has a world food aisle, but you'll never beat the variety and value of shopping at a Chinese or Oriental supermarket. Don't be put off when confronted with brands you have never heard of. If you really want to capture the taste of your local Chinese takeaway or restaurant, you'll need to buy authentic ingredients.

Plan your visit and make a precise list of what you are looking for. You'll be amazed by the huge savings you'll make when buying ingredients. EMBRACE the ADVENTURE. Chinese cooking requires a little understanding but once you learn how to combine tastes and textures, you're on your way to creating perfectly authentic dishes.

There are three ingredients which usually hit a hot wok before anything else. Ginger, garlic and spring onion (the 'Holy Trinity'). They're not always used together, but very often used in different combinations in Chinese cooking, especially Cantonese.

Ginger

The ginger plant originates from southern Asia where the root is used in a variety of dishes. It was one of the first spices exported to Europe from the Far East. Ginger is used in a wide range of food products including candy, biscuits, wine, ale and tea. Always have a large thumb-sized piece of root ginger in your fridge but be sure to check for firmness before using if it's been sitting around for longer than a week. There are other ginger varieties available and your enjoyment of food will always come down to personal taste, but root ginger is the specific variety that gives Chinese cooking its truly authentic flavour.

Garlic

An everyday superfood, this little clove has a distinct pungent and spicy flavour. Native to central Asia it has long been used for seasoning and medicinal purposes, widely believed to be effective against colds, high blood pressure and cholesterol.

The variety of garlic that you choose is very much a personal preference but if using a jumbo bulb, be sure to adjust the quantities in your dish as the recipes are all based on a standard sized bulb. Always look for a firm bulb with no sprouts when shopping for garlic and store in the fridge for up to a week.

Spring onions

Part of the onion family, spring onions have a milder taste than other onions and are widely used across the globe. The entire plant can be used, chopped and added to salads, soups and curries. When shopping for spring onions, choose bunches of fresh un-wilted stems. These will sit happily in the fridge for up to a week but keep them away from the back of the fridge to avoid chill burn.

Oyster sauce

Dark, rich, salty and smooth, this sauce brings a depth of flavour to any dish it is added to and is very often used with vegetables. It's made by slowly cooking oysters until caramelised into a thick, dark brown sauce. You can also buy vegetarian substitutes in most Chinese supermarkets (which may be labelled as 'vegetarian stir-fry sauce').

Lee Kum Kee Premium Oyster Sauce is my brand of choice and is now readily available in many large supermarkets. Store in the fridge after opening.

Sesame oil

Fragrant, smoky and nutty, sesame oil isn't used in the cooking process but rather to season the dish before serving. It is often used in marinades to give the ingredients a nutty note. When buying sesame oil make sure it's pure oil and not blended.

Soy sauce

Probably the most well-known ingredient of Chinese food. Light soy sauce is more commonly used in Chinese cooking to add flavour and saltiness. It is thinner and often used as a light seasoning or for dipping sauces. Dark soy sauce is richer and less salty and might have sugar, such as molasses, added to it. It's often used in marinades and sauces and it adds colour and a sweeter flavour to a dish. Both have a rich umami taste which has been created by the soybean fermentation process.

I prefer to use the Pearl River Bridge brand of soy sauce, both light and dark. Supermarket soy is fine but I would highly recommend going the extra mile in order to achieve that truly authentic flavour.

Fish sauce

Rich, salty and full of flavour, fish sauce is used to replace salt and to add a unique savoury taste to any dish.

Squid Brand is my 'go to' for fish sauce. Opened bottles should be stored in a cool, dark place, but not in the fridge.

Rice vinegar

Slightly sweeter than Western counterparts and not as acidic, rice vinegar is made by fermenting rice or rice wine in China.

Readily available is the Amoy brand which should be stored in a cool, dark but unrefrigerated place.

Chinese rice wine

An alcoholic drink made from rice, not dissimilar to sherry, rice wine has a perfumed bouquet and will give any dish it is added to a distinct Chinese flavour.

Taijade Shaohsing Wine is readily available in most large supermarkets. The average alcohol content of this type of cooking wine is 13.5% and it is not recognised as a beverage. Opened bottles should be stored in a cool, dark cupboard.

Fermented black beans

A widely used seasoning in Chinese cooking, fermented black beans are a must for the store cupboard. Soybeans are left to ferment and as they mature they create a distinct, pungent salty flavour with a rich umami taste.

These are best bought as dried, fermented beans; at your local Oriental supermarket look for the Yang Jiang preserved bean with ginger. Dried beans can be rehydrated in warm water and crushed with the back of a spoon to release their flavour.

Chinese five spice

A blend of star anise, Szechuan peppercorns, cinnamon stick, fennel seeds and cloves. The ingredients are ground to a fine powder to produce a completely unique taste sensation that is warm, aromatic and sweet. See page 29 for how to make your own.

It's well worth a trip to your local Oriental supermarket for a packet of authentic Chinese five spice powder, as although you can buy a variation of this spice mix from most chain supermarkets, you won't get the real Chinese flavour you're looking for. Opened packets should be stored in an airtight container to maintain freshness.

White cornflour (cornstarch)

Widely used in all Asian cooking, it's used to tenderise meats, thicken sauces and soups and coat ingredients before frying.

Groundnut oil

The Chinese use groundnut oil in their cooking as it has a very high smoke point, which means it can get to a higher temperature before it begins to smoke and before the oil starts to degrade and produce harmful compounds. Groundnut oil also has very little flavour so does not interfere with the flavours of the ingredients.

NB People with nut allergies CANNOT use this oil – any other mild-flavoured oils are absolutely fine to use and will not affect your cooking, but be mindful of their lower smoke point when heating your wok or pan.

Rice and noodles

These staple ingredients are great to keep in stock and will stay fresh in airtight containers once opened. Perfect fluffy rice starts with long grain Thai fragrant rice and having dried egg noodles and dried rice vermicelli to hand makes for very quick and easy midweek dinners.

INDEX

ACKNOWLEDGEMENTS

**FAMILY where life begins,
and LOVE never ends!**

This book was such a joy to write, it's basically a glimpse of my life growing up in Mum and Dad's restaurants. Each recipe is a family member and, as I typed, they unlocked the millions of memories I have as a child, surrounded by food; happy, safe, content and full. Maya-Lily and Lola-Rose, my beautiful little Wans, this book is the key to my life growing up, the food I ate and what it means to me. How Nanny and Grandad fed me with love and food, and how both things are the same.

Maya-Lily and Lola-Rose (my beautiful babies), there are no words that could ever come close to telling you how much I love you.

Mum and Dad, where do I start? You have given me so much and taught me that no matter what life throws my way, you will ALWAYS be there to pick me up. I am truly blessed to call you Mum and Dad.

Oilen and Babe (Gok), I often wish we could do it all again. Life was as simple as a Jungle Book T-Shirt and heading to Mum and Dad's restaurant for a bowl of noodles. Nurture taught us that family always comes first, but I didn't need to be taught how to love you.

Clare, you are seriously one hell of an agent. My feet are still running at a million miles an hour since you took a gamble on me.

Sarah Lavelle & Quadrille Publishing, thank you so much for having the confidence to allow me to become one of your authors.

Kwoklyn Wan is a chef and broadcaster. He learnt the tools of his trade working alongside his brother Gok Wan in their family's Cantonese restaurant in Leicester. Kwoklyn now teaches and demos Chinese cooking, and is a martial arts instructor.